Victory Through Discipline

VICTORY THROUGH DISCIPLINE

An Exegetical Commentary on First Corinthians Nine

BY
SPIROS ZODHIATES, TH.D.

AMG
PUBLISHERS
Chattanooga, TN 37422

Victory Through Discipline
An Exegetical Commentary on First Corinthians Nine

ISBN 0-89957-457-2

Printed in the United States of America

03 02 01 00 99 98 –A– 7 6 5 4 3 2

To my beloved nephew Henry Sideropoulos, M.D., M.Div., who has chosen besides his medical profession to also serve Christ, and for this I sincerely congratulate him.

Contents

Preface

The apostle Paul was concerned about using his life to bring honor to Christ and to lead as many souls as possible to acknowledge Him (verses 19–22).

He knew that this would not be accomplished without personal sacrifice. He wanted both his friends and his enemies to know that he was willing to suffer any sacrifice for that purpose. This is why he remained single and why he did not accept compensation for the spiritual work wherein God was pleased to use him in establishing the church in Corinth.

Both friends and enemies were critical of him lest this voluntary privation of privilege would be attributed to a false personal claim that he was a true apostle. This is why he begins this chapter with the defense of his apostolicity.

On the other hand he defends the right of those who work for the gospel to receive compensation for services rendered. Though he goes out of his way to prove that he was worthy of such compensation, he did not permit his conscience to accept it lest there would be some who would point out that what he did he did for the compensation expected.

This was the discipline that he imposed upon himself, and this chapter clearly makes the reason for self-discipline explicit.

Would to God that our motives as pastors and as servants of Christ might be as pure as those of the apostle Paul. His motivating power was not personal need and its satisfaction without disregard of the glory of God, but the greatest possible usefulness as an apostle of Jesus Christ.

The higher our authority and our trust from God, the greater our responsibility of behavior.

I trust that the contents of this book will cause you not only to see the victory that is in Christ, but also to realize that the victory entails discipline and sacrifice. You cannot choose the victories that God promises without voluntarily subjecting yourself to discipline.

SPIROS ZODHIATES

An Overview of First Corinthians

Author:	Paul the apostle, author of thirteen other epistles to various individuals and congregations.
Date:	About A.D. 55.
Recipients:	The congregation Paul had established in Corinth.
Place:	From Ephesus.
Theme:	Paul had received news about the Corinthian brethren from several sources (1 Cor. 1:11; 7:1; 16:17). The church was afflicted with many of the problems that face young churches and new converts. The apostle, under the inspiration of the Holy Spirit, decided to write this urgent letter to admonish and instruct the church. Among other topics he discussed: the necessity of church discipline (5:1–13); divisions and disputes among Christians (1:10–16; 6:1–11); matters of conscience (8:1–13; 10:19–33); the support of preachers (9:1–27); abuses of the Lord's Supper (10:16–17, 21; 11:17–34); the misuse of spiritual gifts (12:1—14:40); and the importance of the resurrection of Jesus Christ (15:1–58).

An Outline of First Corinthians

In the days of the apostle Paul, Corinth was the capital city of the Roman province of Achaia and the glory of Greece. Though its great ancient splendor had been destroyed by the Romans in 120 B.C., the city was rebuilt under Julius Caesar and restored to wealth and luxury under Augustus. Among all the cities of the world, however, it was most well known for its lewdness. The apostle Paul lived in Corinth for eighteen months (Acts 18:11). After his departure, Paul went to Ephesus. During his three-year stay there, he heard reports of wickedness and division within the Corinthian church. In an effort to correct these evils, Paul wrote several letters to them, including the Epistle of First Corinthians.

1:1–9	The introductory remarks of Paul.
1:10–16	Paul condemns the divisions in the church and exhorts its members to unity.
1:17—2:16	Paul defends his ministry. He has preached the wisdom of Christ crucified. This wisdom is foolishness to the world, but is the glory of all those to whom the Spirit of God has revealed the truthfulness of it.
3:1–5	Paul declares that the simplicity of his teaching was due to the carnal state of the Corinthians, which state is clearly evidenced by their divisions.
3:6–23	Jesus Christ is the only foundation. Ministers are mere servants; the work is God's.
4:1–6	The duty of ministers is faithfulness.
4:6–21	Paul contrasts the arrogance and conceit of the false teachers to the humility and sacrifice of the apostles. Using his unique position as their spiritual father, Paul calls on the Corinthian believers to be discerning.
5:1–13	Flagrant, sexual immorality was being practiced by one of the members of the congregation. Paul reproves

	their lack of discipline and calls for expulsion of the guilty party.
6:1–11	Christians should not bring their legal disputes before heathen judges.
6:12–20	Paul reprimands the perversion of the principle of Christian liberty to excuse fornication. Our bodies belong to the Lord and should be devoted to His glory.
7:1–17	Paul answers their questions about marriage.
7:18–24	Paul advises that, provided they are not immoral or unlawful, our social positions should remain intact after coming to Christ.
7:25–40	Paul answers their questions about virgins and widows.
8:1–13	Christian liberty and conscience: was it lawful to eat meat that had been sacrificed to false gods?
9:1–23	Paul declares the right of ministers to be faithfully supported by their congregation.
9:24—10:13	Exhortations to self-denial.
10:14—11:1	While the purchase of meat offered to idols is a matter of conscience, attendance at the heathen feasts of sacrifice is idolatry, even if such was not their intention.
11:2–16	Men and women should take care to conform to the customs of dress in their community that assure modesty and properly reflect the man to be "the glory of God" and the woman to be "the glory of the man."
11:17–34	Paul exhorts the Corinthians to properly partake of the Lord's Supper.
12:1–31	Paul answers their questions about spiritual gifts. He reminds them that they are all members of one body. God has distributed these gifts so that each member may perform the function it is designed for.

13:1–13	Love [*agápe* {26}] is superior to all other gifts.
14:1–25	The gift of prophecy is more valuable than the gift of tongues.
14:26–40	Principles for orderly public worship.
15:1–34	Paul proves the fact of the resurrection of Christ. It is the foundation of our faith and the surety of our own resurrection.
15:35–58	Paul explains the nature of our resurrection.
16:1–9	Paul's specific instructions for the collection of monies from several Greek congregations for the poverty-stricken saints in Palestine.
16:10–12	Recommendations for Timothy and Apollos to be accepted by the Corinthians.
16:13–24	Paul's final admonition to them to stand firm in the faith. Salutation.

1 Cor. 9:1 | *Christian Liberty*

Am I not free? Am I not an apostle? Have I not seen Jesus Christ our Lord? Are you not the result of my work in the Lord?

The apostle Paul begins the ninth chapter with a series of rhetorical questions to which the answer is a resounding "Yes!" The reason for the necessity of an affirmative answer is due to the nature of the questions being asked with the absolute "not" (*ouk* [3756]) in verses 1, 2, 4, 5, 6, 8, and 13.

"Am I Not Free?"

Some Greek texts such as the UBS and Nestle's Text have the question "Am I not free?" preceding "Am I not an apostle?" In the KJV, which is a translation of the TR, the question of freedom is second. I prefer the question regarding Paul's apostolicity to follow that of his freedom in Christ. Paul's response to "Am I not an apostle?" is in defense of his affirmative claim that he has seen the Lord. Therefore, we consider the first question to be that of his freedom in Christ.

We must associate this ninth chapter of 1 Corinthians with chapters 8 and 10 as being related with the total discussion regarding Christian freedom. Paul maintains he must obey his own conscience in choosing whether or not to eat meats sacrificed to idols.

It is noteworthy that in 1 Corinthians 8:9 the word that is translated "liberty" (KJV, RSV) or "freedom" (NIV) is the word *exousía* (1849), the meaning of which is authority, the right and the power. The word, however, from which "free" is translated in 1 Corinthians 9:1 is *eleútheros* (1658). In Galatians 5:1 the apostle Paul says, "Stand fast therefore in the liberty [*eleuthería* {1657}, freedom] wherewith Christ has made us free [*ēleuthérōse*, the aorist active indicative, third person singular of *eleutheróō* {1659}, to free, liberate], and be not entangled again with the yoke of bondage [*douleías*, the genitive of *douleía* {1397}, slavery, bondage]." A freed man is one who was in bondage and has been set free. This is the state of every born-again believer in Jesus Christ. In the state of unbelief we were slaves (*doúloi*, the plural of *doúlos* [1401], slave) of sin (Rom. 6:17). The state of the believer, however, is presented as being a slave of God. "You were made slaves [*edoulṓthēte*, the plural aorist passive indicative of *doulóō* {1402}, to enslave, to make a slave] of righteousness" (Rom. 6:18, 22). That is the true state of freedom. This state of freedom is also called slavery to righteousness (Rom. 6:18). Righteousness is doing that which is right in our relationships with God and with others. In this freedom, the believer does not seek excuses for sin (1 Pet. 2:16).

Freedom to Make Choices

In his freedom, a believer can make choices within the community of other believers. In varying degrees he can exercise his rights and privileges which may be called *exousía*, authority, privilege. The choices that he makes in the context of 1 Corinthians 8—10 have their rewards. The Christian is never permitted to be selfish, but the degree in which he shows his altruism may be great or small. It may involve personal privation and sacrifice, or he may give out of his abundance (2 Cor. 8:1–7). It is this same word *exousía*, authority, that is used in 1 Corinthians 8:9; 9:4–6, 12, 18.

This chapter is an elaboration of 1 Corinthians 8:9: "But take heed lest by any means this liberty [*exousía*] of yours becomes a stumblingblock to them that are weak." Already Paul has stated that his freedom in Christ finds its expression in love. One is free in Christ, "For he that is called in the Lord, being a servant, is the Lord's freeman; likewise also he that is called, being free, is Christ's servant" (1 Cor. 7:22). The word "servant" in this text is *doúlos* (1401), slave. He who has been made free is a slave of Christ to do His will and to serve others even as Christ did. What is translated as being "free" is the Greek word *eleútheros* (1658), free or liberated. This is diametrically the opposite of a slave, but in this context, it is a synonym of being a slave of Christ. In other words, the apostle Paul is stating that the really free man is the one who has been enslaved by Christ. This is exactly what he means in 1 Corinthians 9:19 when he states, "For though I be free from all men, yet have I made myself a servant unto all, that I might gain the more," meaning, I surrendered my freedom to become a slave of Christ, and in my slavery to Him, I have been able to win more to Him.

The ultimate objective is not the enjoyment of our freedom, but the salvation of other souls (1 Cor. 9:22). Paul is saying that in his Christian life, he is free to live as he wants to, but his nature is such that he wants to do only that which pleases Christ (2 Pet. 1:4). Each Christian must live his own life of pleasing the Lord; one cannot determine the life that other Christians are to live. As Paul says in Romans 14:5, ". . . let every man be fully persuaded in his own mind." What is translated "let every man" is the Greek adjective *hékastos* (1538), each one referring to each separate individual. "Be fully persuaded" translates the Greek verb *plērophoreísthō,* the present passive imperative, third person singular of *plērophoréō* (4135), to assure fully. The present tense indicates that one should always be fully assured that what he is doing is acceptable to God. We should not make decisions on the spur of the moment as guided by circumstances, but we should have principles of a lifestyle as guided by a godly philosophy of life. And then Paul adds, "in his own mind." This is translated from *en tṓ idíō noḯ* (*en* [1722], in; *tṓ*, the dative masculine singular article of *ho* [3588], the; *idíō,* the dative masculine singular of the adjective *ídios* [2398], his own, as pertaining to a private person, an individual; *noḯ* [3563], the dative masculine singular of the noun *noús* [3563] mind). A Christian is free, but his freedom is enslaved by the love of Christ. However, in that context of love, each Christian as an individual has to exercise his own mental powers in intelligent judgments. The freedom of an enlightened Christian is freedom to demonstrate the love of Christ to others, and freedom not to retaliate when he has been harmed. Paul very emphatically insists on the necessity of qualifying the exercise of one's own liberty in regard to the claims of others and, especially, his brother with whom he has fellowship (1 Cor. 8:13). The believer's freedom must not involve harm to others or an infringement upon their liberty. Self-limitation for the sake of others is, indeed, an example of the truest exercise of freedom.

It is difficult for the Christian to develop a wise and godly philosophy of the exercise of his freedom. He is given the right (*exousía,* authority) of free action in the common affairs of life, such as choosing what and how much food he may eat, whether to marry and whom to marry, what work to do and what the expected compensation should be (1 Cor. 9:4–6, 12).

Individual Choices Entail Personal Accountability

According to 1 Corinthians 8:9, the Christian should take heed lest by any means his liberty becomes a stumblingblock to the weak. This liberty of the Christian is both fundamental and fragile. Each man has to "work out his own salvation" (Phil. 2:12), to be "fully assured in his own mind" (Rom. 14:5) to give account of himself to God (Rom. 14:12). Note that the accounting that the Christian must give to the Lord is individual and personal. The word *hékastos,* each one, is used in Romans 14:12 which would confirm that the New Testament stresses not only individual choice, but also individual accountability. Christians are the free citizens of the heavenly Jerusalem. They are children of liberty (Gal. 4:26). This abiding freedom is given by Christ Himself (Gal. 5:1). He calls Christians into liberty (Gal. 5:13). Henceforth, they are not bound by past traditions nor by laws or rites that can bind them. When Moses is read, it shall be with no fear of the letter of the law (2 Cor. 3:15–18), but in the reverent freedom of the spirit (2 Cor. 3:6–8). The disciple feels himself freed from that yoke (Acts 15:10). He has been led into a larger world where "the liberty which we have in Christ Jesus" is prized (Gal. 2:4). The escape has been from the bondage of a religion of fear into the liberty of faith that discerns in God the eternal Fatherhood (Rom. 8:15). So Paul prays that the Word may have free course, may run, spreading the gospel far and wide with an unhindered spirit (2 Thess. 3:1), and may leave each worker to develop his own method (1 Cor. 9:1) and rules of conduct, "For why is my liberty judged by another man's conscience?" (1 Cor. 10:29).

Freedom to Choose Is Not License to Do Evil

A Christian's liberty implies a limitation. He is to be "as free, yet not using his liberty for a cloak of maliciousness, but as the bond-servant of God" (1 Pet. 2:16). The bond-servant is free to please his master who freed him. He has no part with those worldly practices so characterizing the bond-servants of corruption (2 Pet. 2:19). He knows that he will be judged in his speech and conduct by the law of liberty which has taken the place of the ancient law of do's and do not's (James 2:12). Being made free from sin, he is still a servant, but of righteousness, a "servant to God" (Rom. 6:18, 20, 22), and from the "bondage of corruption," he has entered into the "liberty of the glory of the children of God" (Rom. 8:21). This liberty is the exchange of a hateful enslavement for a precious bondage. The literal slave has now become "the Lord's freedman [*apeleútheros* {558}, an emancipated slave]," whereas the free man now becomes "Christ's bond-servant" (1 Cor. 7:21, 22). That service is the ministry to others, a bondage into which Paul boasts and glories that he had brought himself (1 Cor. 9:19). He has found a new law in place of the ancient prohibitory "law of sin and of death," and this law of the spirit of life in Christ Jesus has made him free (Rom. 8:2).

The apostle Paul is not only declaring that he is a free man, but he also declares in Galatians 5:1 that his freedom was due to what Christ did for him. He says, "Stand fast, therefore, in the liberty wherewith Christ has made us free, and be not entangled again with the yoke of bondage."

From What Was Paul Freed?

The apostle Paul was not only certain who made him free, but also from what He freed him. In 1 Corinthians 9:19 he writes, "For though I be free from **all men,** yet have I made myself servant unto all, that I might gain the more." In the Greek text it says, "For though I be free from all. . . ." The word "men" has been added by the translators. Paul was referring not only to all men who sought to enslave him, but also to all the vices that would have the same effect on him. When he writes, "I am free," in effect he was saying what he said to the Corinthians in 1 Corinthians 6:11: "And such were some of you, but you are washed, but you are sanctified, but you are justified in the name of the Lord Jesus, and by the Spirit of our God."

Does he delineate the evils from which he was freed? Yes, indeed, and it will be good for us to find out all the evils from which Paul was liberated.

Free From the Bondage of the Law

The first freedom that Paul experienced was from the bondage of the law. He speaks of this freedom in his letters to the Romans and Galatians. He came to the conclusion that not only he as a Jewish believer, but also all Jewish believers and Gentiles, were free from the obligation to observe the Jewish law in its particular institutions and ceremonial rules. The old sacrificial system was abolished. Christians, according to Romans 2:15, by believing on the Lord Jesus Christ, "show the work of the law written in their hearts, their conscience also bearing witness, and their thoughts the meanwhile accusing or else excusing one another." And in Romans 3:20 he writes, "Therefore, by the deeds of the law there shall no flesh be justified in His sight: for by the law is the knowledge of sin." And in verse 28 he says, "Therefore we conclude that a man is justified by faith without the deeds of the law." The law could condemn them only, but could not redeem them as Christ did "because the law works wrath: for where no law is, there is no transgression" (Rom. 4:15). Triumphantly Paul declares the Christian's freedom from the Law when he says in Romans 6:14: "For sin shall not have dominion over you: for you are not under the law, but under grace." That Paul was freed from the ceremonial requirements of the Mosaic Law for redemptive purposes is declared in Romans 10:4: "For Christ is the end of the law for righteousness to everyone that believes." And then in Galatians 2:16 he writes: "Knowing that a man is not justified by the works of the law, but by the faith of Jesus Christ, even we have believed in Jesus Christ, that we might be justified by the faith of Christ, and not by the works of the law: for by the works of the law shall no flesh be justified." And in 3:13 Paul also writes: "Christ has redeemed us from the curse of the law, being made a curse for us: for it is written, 'Cursed is everyone that hangs on a tree.' "

What then was the purpose of the law? It is stated in Galatians 3:19, "Wherefore then serves the law? It was added because of transgressions, till the seed [Christ] should come to whom the promise was made; and it was ordained by angels in the hand of a mediator." And then Paul asks in verse 21: "Is the law then against the promises of God? God forbid: for if there had been a law given which could have given life, verily righteousness should have been by the law." The conclusion of the purpose of the law is stated in verse 24: "Wherefore the law was our schoolmaster to bring us unto Christ, that we might be justified by faith."

How then can we fulfill the law? Paul tells us in Galatians 6:2, "Bear ye one another's burdens, and so fulfill the law of Christ." The law is fulfilled by Christians through love that He implants in their hearts (1 John 5:1). The law had only condemnation of the sinner, but not his redemption (Rom. 7). Paul does not take an attitude against the law, but speaks of it as having fulfilled its purpose which now is taken over by Christ. "Wherefore the law is holy, and the commandment holy, and just, and good" (Rom. 7:12). As Christ says in Matthew 5:17, "Think not that I am come to destroy the law, or the prophets: I am not come to destroy, but to fulfill."

The apostle James is in full agreement with Paul when he says that the believer is not governed by a law regulating his life, but by a law of liberty (James 1:25). This is the law of freedom that Jesus Christ promises when He says in John 8:36, "If the Son therefore shall make you free, you shall be free indeed." This is freedom from slavery to sin and an identity of character with that of Christ. It is such an intimate conformity with the mind and desire of Christ that "whatever we ask, we receive of Him, because we keep His commandments, and do those things that are pleasing in His sight. And this is His commandment, that we should believe on the name of His Son Jesus Christ, and love one another, as He gave us commandment" (1 John 3:22, 23). Furthermore, in Galatians 6:2 Paul calls the law of God "the law of Christ" which can be fulfilled only as we bear one another's burdens.

Being made free by Christ entails some negative aspects through the positive of loving your neighbor as yourself as Paul states in Romans 13:9, 10: "For this, you shall not commit adultery, you shall not kill, you shall not steal, you shall not bear false witness, you shall not covet; and if there be any other commandment, it is briefly comprehended in this saying, namely, you shall love your neighbor as yourself. Love works no ill to his neighbor: therefore, love is the fulfilling of the law." It is the love of Christ that made Paul state in 1 Corinthians 8:13, "Wherefore, if meat makes my brother to offend, I will eat no flesh while the world stands, lest I make my brother to offend."

Free From the Bondage of Sin

When Paul declared his freedom in Christ, he declared his freedom not only from the Law of Moses, but also from the bondage of sin. Jesus Christ expressed in no uncertain terms that sin enslaves when He said in John 8:34, "Whoever commits sin is the servant [*doúlos*, slave] of sin." Unredeemed man is presented as a slave of sin in Romans 6:17, 18: "But God be thanked that you were the slaves of sin, but you have obeyed from the heart that form of doctrine which was delivered you. Being then **made free from sin**, you became the slaves of righteousness." It is therefore clear that "he that commits sin [as a lifestyle] is of the devil; for the devil sins from the beginning. For this purpose the Son of God was manifested that He might destroy the works of the devil. Whoever is born of God does not commit sin [continuously]; for his seed remains in him: and he cannot sin [continuously], because he is born of God" (1 John 3:8, 9).

Jesus Christ taught that fulfilling all the commandments of the law is loving the Lord unconditionally and one's neighbor as himself (Matt. 22:34–40). Paul's philosophy of life can be summed up in what he wrote in Romans 13:10: "Love works no ill to his neighbor: therefore love is the fulfillment of the law." This is why in 1 Corinthians 8:13 he says, "Wherefore, if meat make my brother to offend, I will eat no flesh while the world standeth, lest I make my brother to offend."

Free From the Bondage of Idolatry

There is a third freedom which Paul declares that he possesses. It is the freedom from the bondage of idolatry. We have to remember that Paul was a converted Jew living in the midst of people recently freed from idolatry, that is, the Gentiles. Therefore, he writes to them in Galatians 4:8, 9: "How is it, then, when you knew not God, you did service [*edouleúsate*, the aorist active indicative, second person plural of *douleúō* {1398}, to serve as if in bondage as slaves] unto them [idols] which by nature are not gods. But now, after you have known God, or rather are known of God, how do you turn again to the weak and beggarly elements, whereunto you desire again to be in bondage?"

Sufferings Inherent in the Age in Which We Live

As Christians, it will help us to consider those things from which we are not liberated in this earthly life of ours.

First, as redeemed believers, we are not exempted from the general sufferings of this earthly existence. Such suffering falls into two categories. In Romans 8:18 Paul calls them "the sufferings of this age" or season (*kairoú,* the genitive of *kairós* [2540], season, meaning our earthly life). The Lord Jesus Christ suffered, not because of His own sin, but because He became sin for us. Christ was not a sinner (Heb. 4:15); nevertheless He died for our sins (1 Cor. 15:3). We, on the other hand, suffer and die because of our sinful nature inherited from Adam (Rom. 5:12). While during our life we can have victory in Christ, we cannot escape the consequences of our sin manifested in our bodily existence. We now have in our present redemption "the first fruits of the Spirit" (Rom. 8:23). While on this earth, "we groan within ourselves, waiting for the adoption, that is to say, the redemption of our body" (Romans 8:23b). Christ paid the price for our sin on the cross, and now we have the redemption of our spirits with victory over the sufferings of our bodies. He died, however, once and for all for the final redemption of our bodies that is yet to come. Therefore, we suffer not just because of our sins, but because we have a sinful nature inherited from Adam and are not free from the consequences of darkness nor sin. In the New Testament this is called *skotía* (4653), the consequences of darkness (see author's comment on 1 John 1:5 in his book *The Epistles of John*), and thus we are not free from the suffering and corruptibility of the body. This will come to us as a gift of redemption at the time of the resurrection when we obtain our resurrection bodies (1 Cor. 15:42, 50).

Sufferings We Incur for Christ's Sake

Secondly, believers are not exempt from suffering for the sake of Christ. This is voluntary suffering which we are willing to endure when we become crucified with Christ. When Paul states that he is a free man, he does not say that he expects to live on a bed of roses. He knew that he must continue to live in a sinful world which still waits for its redemption (Rom. 8:19–22).

As Christ emptied Himself and became in the likeness of man (Phil. 2:6–8), so we must suffer with Him in the accomplishment of His mission through us (Acts 26:23; Luke 24:26). Only as our Lord was willing to endure whatever human experience might come to Him could He reveal the Father and help turn men to righteousness by showing them the enormity of sin (Heb. 13:12). "Though He were a Son, yet learned He obedience by the things which He suffered; and being made perfect, He became the author of eternal salvation unto all them that obey Him" (Heb. 5:8, 9). Through His heroic, victorious endurance of sin-imposed suffering, He became our High Priest, able to succor those who are tempted (Heb. 2:17, 18; 4:15). In this noble sense, the sufferings of Christ are central to the gospel, and Peter could justly say that he was a witness of the sufferings of Christ (1 Pet. 5:1). The followers of Christ are not free from the experiences which He voluntarily endured in His incarnation and which we must assume in our redemption.

> Remember the word that I said unto you, "The servant is not greater than his lord." If they have persecuted me, they will also persecute you; if they have kept my saying, they will keep yours also. But all these things will they do unto you for my name's sake, because they know not him that sent me (John 15:20, 21).

Although Christ promised life more abundantly, it was not a life free from suffering for the sake of Christ (John 10:10; 16:33). In fact, the believers' relationship to Him may cause them to suffer as He did. If they are faithful to Him, the enmity and opposition He met with will also, to some extent, fall to their lot. Paul, who endured so much on behalf of the gospel (2 Cor. 11:22–33), with reason could speak of sharing the sufferings of Christ. "The sufferings of Christ abound in us," he says in 2 Corinthians 1:5. He longed to know "the fellowship of His sufferings" (Phil. 3:10).

While those who belong to Christ also suffer with Him, those who thus suffer will share His glory also (Rom. 8:17). "Inasmuch as you are partakers of Christ's sufferings, rejoice" (1 Pet. 4:13). "If we suffer, we shall also reign with him" (2 Tim. 2:12). When Paul was chosen, the Lord said, ". . . for I will show him how great things he must suffer for my name's sake" (Acts 9:16). Paul did indeed, but he says, "for the which cause I also suffer these things: nevertheless I am not ashamed: for I know whom I have believed and am persuaded that He is able to keep that which I have committed unto him against that day" (2 Tim. 1:12). One cannot be free from suffering if he is an apostle and teacher. Accordingly, Paul expects Timothy to endure hardship with him (2 Tim. 2:3). "Be not ashamed of the testimony of our Lord, nor of me his prisoner: but suffer the hardship of the gospel" (2 Tim. 1:8). "Suffer hardship, do the work of an evangelist" (2 Tim. 4:5). Paul suffered and was shamefully treated at Philippi (1 Thess. 2:2). There he endured stripes and imprisonment (Acts 16:19–23, especially v. 23). He also suffered because of the misunderstanding of his converts in believing that the items used had miraculous powers (Acts 19:12), and many of his converts frequently suffered on account of their faith. The Galatians suffered many things (cf. Acts 14:2–5, 19–22). The Philippians suffered on behalf of Christ (Phil.

1:29). The Thessalonians suffered for the kingdom of God (2 Thess. 1:5) at the hands of their fellow countrymen, as the churches of Judea did at the hands of the Jews (1 Thess. 2:14). The recipients of 1 Peter also suffered wrongfully in well-doing (1 Pet. 2:19, 20), for righteousness' sake (1 Pet. 3:14, cf. v. 17), and as Christians (1 Pet. 4:16). Peter told them that those who were called to God's eternal kingdom in Christ may suffer (1 Pet. 5:10), just as Paul had told Timothy that "all that would live godly in Christ Jesus shall suffer persecution" (2 Tim. 3:12). Among the things which the Christians of Smyrna had to suffer was imprisonment (Rev. 2:10, cf. Heb. 13:3). The Hebrews are reminded that after they were enlightened they "endured a great conflict of sufferings; partly being made a gazing stock both by reproaches and by afflictions, and partly, becoming partakers with them that were so used" (Heb. 10:32, 33). The heroes of faith also suffered for their faithfulness. Moses preferred to suffer affliction with the people of God (Heb. 11:25). The prophets gave an example of suffering (James 5:10). The early Christians seem to have worried little about what we call the problem of suffering, except perhaps, insofar as their sufferings were ascribed to the activity of the devil (1 Pet. 5:9). Their chief concern seems to have been that they should suffer according to the will of God (1 Pet. 4:19), that is, for well doing (1 Pet. 3:17).

Thus when the apostle Paul says, "I am free," he did not mean he was free from the privilege of suffering for his brethren, especially the ones he was trying to influence for Christ. It behooves us to be assured from what we are freed and from what we dare not become free. We should never consider ourselves to be free to enjoy that which will become a stumblingblock to our brethren (1 Cor. 8:9, 13).

"Am I Not an Apostle?"

The second rhetorical question which Paul asks that demands a positive answer is, "Am I not an apostle?" Each of these questions begins with the absolute "not" (*ou* [3756]), which takes the consonant *k* (*ouk*) because the next word begins with a vowel. The expected answers are, Of course I am a free man; of course I am an apostle. This is not the first and only time that Paul claims to be an apostle of Jesus Christ. He begins his epistle by saying, "Paul, called to be an apostle of Jesus Christ through the will of God" (1 Cor. 1:1).

What did Paul mean by the word "apostle" (*apóstolos* [652], a delegate, a messenger)? The word has both a narrow and a broader meaning in the New Testament. The narrow meaning applies to the twelve disciples of Christ who are named in Matthew 10:2–4, Mark 3:16–19, and Luke 6:12–16. The suicide of Judas led to the appointment by lot by the remaining disciples of Matthias to fill his place (Acts 1:23–26). Matthias was selected because he fulfilled the conditions of an apostle in that he was with Christ and the disciples from the time of the baptism of John until he witnessed the resurrected Christ (Acts 1:21, 22). Apostleship, however, was not a man-appointed office, but a direct commissioning by the Lord. We thus do not see the Lord accepting Matthias into the group of the Twelve Apostles in lieu of Judas.

Rather, through a personal, supernatural, and exceptional calling, the Lord appointed another man to whom He appeared after His resurrection and His ascension. This was Saul of Tarsus. Saul was not a friend of Jesus, but rather an enemy who took part in the judicial murder of Stephen, the first martyr of the Christian church. He was the only enemy of Christ to whom the Lord showed Himself after His resurrection and ascension. Saul, along with the others, did not see what Stephen saw—the heavens opening up and the Son of man standing on the right hand of God (Acts 7:55, 56). Little did he realize, however, as he was traveling to Damascus from Jerusalem to arrest and imprison Christians, that he was going to have a similar experience with Christ Jesus appearing to him (Acts 9:1–9). Saul was a convinced unbeliever fighting against the truth. He became an example, however, of the irresistible grace of God. Perhaps the appearance of the Lord Jesus to him was for the purpose of showing us that God has peculiar ways whereby He can call people and can save them: no one is beyond His grace. This gives us the faith to persevere in prayer for the lost, no matter how hardened they are.

In Romans 1:1 and 1 Corinthians 1:1, Paul speaks of himself as a "called apostle" (*klētós* [2822], the nominative masculine singular adjective of *kaléō* {2564}, to call; *apóstolos,* apostle). He was not only called supernaturally to be an apostle, but also his very calling to become a believer was supernatural. The appearance of the risen and ascended Christ gave birth to faith in Him and service also to the One who saved him.

"Have I Not Seen Jesus Christ Our Lord?"

The beholding of the Lord Jesus Christ after His resurrection was one of the qualifications of a true apostle. The first thing that we must determine is the meaning of the verb used here. It is *heṓraka*, the perfect active indicative, first person singular of *horáō* (3708), meaning to see. Primarily, it means to see with the eyes. Paul did not see the risen Christ in a dream or mentally, but with his own eyes, and He appeared to him in a form that was recognizable, in bodily form. Undoubtedly Paul knew Him. In this respect, it is synonymous with the verb *blépō* (991), to see with the eyes. But *horáō* also has the meaning of mental perception (Rom. 15:21; Col. 2:18). In other words, when Paul saw the human figure of Christ appear to him, not only did he see with his eyes, but he understood with his mind that this form was Jesus who walked on the streets of Palestine, and that it was He, undoubtedly, with whom he was acquainted. It was true that Paul did not see Christ when He was walking on this earth after His resurrection. It is very likely, though, that he saw the Lord before His resurrection during the days he was a persecutor of the church. Paul, called Saul at that time, kept the garments of those who were stoning Stephen to death (Acts 7:58). As the risen Christ was seen by Stephen standing at the right hand of God (Acts 7:55, 56), so He was seen by the persecutor Saul.

An essential element of being an apostle was to be a witness of the resurrection of the Lord Jesus. Peter in his Pentecostal address said, "This Jesus God has raised up, whereof we are all witnesses" (Acts 2:32), and in Acts 3:15 the same apostle says, "And [you] killed the Prince of Life, whom God has raised from the dead; whereof we are witnesses." Then in Acts 4:33 we read, "And with great power did the apostles witness of the resurrection of the Lord Jesus: and great grace was upon them all."

Evidently Matthias was chosen to be counted among the twelve to take the place of Judas, since apparently he was a witness of the resurrected Lord Jesus (Acts 1:22).

In 1 Corinthians 15, the apostle Paul equates the appearance of the Lord Jesus after His resurrection to himself as being of the same value as His appearance to the Twelve, and to Cephas, that is, Peter, in particular (1 Cor. 15:4–9).

After the death, resurrection, and ascension of the Lord Jesus, He appeared only to believers. But there was one exception, and this was the great persecutor of the gospel, Saul of Tarsus. The apostle likens his vision of as one who is born out of "due time" (*éktrōma*, [1626], miscarriage, abnormal birth). He did not serve and love the Lord while the Lord was ministering here on earth. However, the verb used for his appearance to the other apostles (*ṓphthē,* the aorist passive indicative, third person singular of *horáō*, to see) is used also in the Lord's appearance to Paul himself (1 Cor. 15:7, 8).

Jesus Was Actually Seen and Recognized by Paul

The experience that Paul had in seeing the Lord Jesus after His resurrection must be distinguished from the experiences which he had at other times. Such a one is found in Acts 18:9 in Corinth, when, under persecution, the Lord appeared to Paul in the night by a vision and said to him, "Be not afraid, but speak, and hold not your peace" (Acts 18:9).

At another time, when Paul was being pressed by a persecuting mob in Jerusalem (Acts 22:17, 18) while he prayed in the temple, he saw the Lord in a trance (*ekstásei*, the dative feminine singular of the noun *ékstasis* [1611], amazement). In this, the Lord warned Paul to hurry and leave Jerusalem, for the mob was not going to receive his testimony concerning Jesus Christ.

There was yet another time when the Lord appeared to Paul, and this was when He called him into paradise to assure him in regard to his physical afflictions that God's grace was sufficient for him (2 Cor. 12:1–10).

When Ananias received Paul in Damascus, no more a persecutor but a believer, he "putting his hands on Paul said, 'Brother Saul, the Lord, even Jesus, that appeared unto you in the way as you came, has sent me, that you might receive your sight, and be filled with the Holy Ghost'" (Acts 9:17). The word translated "that appeared" is *ophtheís*, the aorist passive participle, nominative masculine singular of *horáō*, to see and to perceive, the same verb as is used consistently in 1 Corinthians 15:5–8. When Paul went to Jerusalem, it is said in Acts 9:27, "But Barnabas took him, and brought him to the apostles, and declared unto them how he had seen [*eíde*, the aorist active indicative, third person singular of *eídon*, the aorist of *horáō*, to see physically and perceptually] the Lord in the way."

Nowhere else does the apostle Paul use the expression, "I have seen [*heōraka*] Jesus the Lord."

The TR and the MT read, "Have I not seen Jesus **Christ** our Lord?" The UBS, however, has, "Have I not seen Jesus our Lord?" It omits "Christ" (*Christón*). I prefer the TR as the genuine text, for Paul then would consistently refer to Jesus of history as being the Christ of God and the Lord (1 Cor. 8:6; Rom. 1:1; 1 Cor. 1:1; 2 Cor. 1:1; Gal. 1:1; Eph. 1:1).

Paul, in his defense before the throng in Jerusalem, spoke of his experience of Christ on the road to Damascus and reiterated the message sent to him through Ananias: "The God of our fathers has chosen you that you should know His will, and see that Just One, and should hear the voice of His mouth" (Acts 22:14). There is no doubt that Paul saw a figure in heaven, the same as the figure of Jesus while on earth speaking to him in a language that he could understand. This is corroborated by the account we find in Acts 9:3–6:

> And as he journeyed, he came near Damascus: and suddenly there shone around about him a light from heaven: and he fell to the earth, and heard a voice saying unto him, "Saul, Saul, why do you persecute me?" And he said, "Who are you Lord?" And the Lord said, "I am Jesus whom you persecute: it is hard for you to kick against the pricks." And he trembling and astonished said, "Lord, what will you have me to do?" And the Lord said unto him, "Arise, and go into the city, and it shall be told you what you must do."

So the Lord not only appeared to Saul, who knew that He was Jesus the Christ his Lord, but He also spoke with him.

"Are You Not My Work in the Lord?"

Paul further defends his apostolicity by posing another question which demands an affirmative answer. The work of Paul in

Corinth is reported in Acts 18:1–17. He labored there for eighteen months and considered himself as a father to the Corinthian believers (1 Cor. 4:15). It was a great sorrow to Paul that some of the Corinthians were still unrepentant in spite of the fact that while he was in Corinth, his ministry was accompanied by signs and wonders and mighty deeds in demonstration of his apostleship (see 2 Cor. 12:12, 21).

A little phrase that Paul adds, "in the Lord," is very important to note, lest we think that he had inherent power as an apostle. It was only in the power and by the enablement of the Lord that he was able to accomplish anything in Corinth. It is as if he were repeating what we find in 1 Corinthians 3:5–7, "Who then is Paul, and who is Apollos, but ministers by whom you believed, even as the Lord gave to every man? I have planted, Apollos watered; but God gave the increase. So then neither is he that planted anything, neither he that watered; but God has given the increase." Then, in verse 9, he adds, "For we are laborers together with God: you are God's husbandry, you are God's building." The phrases, "God gave the increase" and "God has given the increase," use the Greek verb *auxánō* (837) which means to grow, to sprout into life. No increase (*aúxēsis* [838], growth) can occur without the divinely-caused element of life. The Word of God is the living seed (*spóros* [4703], seed, or *spérma* [4690], sperm; see Matt. 13:38; Luke 8:11). If it were not for the life that is in the seed, there would be no increase at all in spite of any human effort, even if apostolic.

<u>LESSONS:</u>

1. The apostle Paul repeatedly declares that he is a slave of Christ (Rom. 1:1).
2. However, being a slave of Christ, he is free to choose between what is good and what is excellent within that will. Whereas he was formerly

the slave of sin, now being a slave of Christ, he is free to do righteousness (Rom. 6:20–22).

3. As an apostle, he was chosen, yet he had the freedom to accept God's choice for himself. In Romans 1:1 and 1 Corinthians 1:1, he is called "chosen" (*klētós* [2822]). The word *klētós* has a meaning of "appointed," one chosen out and empowered to do a certain work for which he is fitted and enabled. It is equivalent to *eklektós* (1588), the adjective form of *eklégomai* (1586), to effectively choose out of. The apostle Paul claimed to be so chosen and appointed.
4. In support of his call, he stated that he saw and perceived Jesus after His resurrection (Acts 9:27; 22:17–21; 26:13, 14).
5. Part of his work was the establishment of the church in Corinth.
6. However, he gives the glory and the effectiveness of the work to the Lord by adding the phrase "in the Lord."

1 Cor. 9:2 | Evidence of Paul's Apostolicity

If to others I am not an apostle, nevertheless to you I am: for you are the seal of my apostleship in the Lord.

If it were not for the human efforts of the apostle Paul sealed by God's Spirit, there would not have been a Christian church in sinful Corinth. The work that he did in Corinth had its rewards and its heartaches. We are told in Acts 18:8 that "Crispus, the chief ruler of the synagogue, believed on the Lord with all his house; and many of the Corinthians hearing believed and were baptized." It must have been very rewarding to Paul to see Crispus and his family come to believe, in spite of his initial objection and persecution of the gospel. To encourage him, the Lord spoke to Paul in the form of a vision, "Be not afraid, but speak, and hold not your peace: for I am with you, and no man shall set on you to hurt you: for I have much people in this city" (Acts 18:9, 10). So Paul persevered.

"If to Others I Am Not an Apostle"

It was not long before the Corinthian church experienced a division, and there were various parties recognizing the leadership of men such as Apollo, Cephas, and Paul. They even had established a party of Christ (1 Cor. 1:12). This caused great sorrow to Paul, so he asked a question in 1 Corinthians 1:13: "Is Christ divided? Was Christ crucified for you? Or were you baptized in the name of Paul?" Then he answers his own question by saying, "I thank God that I baptized none of you, but Crispus and Gaius, lest any should say that I have baptized in my own name" (vv. 14, 15). Paul baptized Crispus who was the chief ruler of the synagogue in Corinth. This is why, in both verses 1 and 2 of the ninth chapter when Paul speaks of the Corinthians being his work, he is very careful to add "in the Lord." He was, indeed, an apostle among them, but always "in the Lord."

Besides the presence of factions that arose in Corinth, there were those who called themselves superapostles (2 Cor. 11:5; 12:11). These must have been those leaders who wanted to assume the preeminence among the Corinthian believers. They claimed authoritarian rule and did not allow the believers to exercise the freedom of conscience for which Paul, a true apostle, argues so admirably in 1 Corinthians 8:8–10. These superapostles evidently attempted to deny Paul the right of apostleship. So they must be the "others" to whom he is referring in this verse. This, however, is a supposition that he makes to defend his own apostleship. He claims that he has the right of apostleship by also having done the pioneer work among the Corinthian Christians. He says, "If [*ei* {1487}, the subjective suppositional conjunction 'if'] to others I am not an apostle." It may be, he says, that I am not an apostle to those who have formed their own party and to the superapostles, but I ought to be to you, the true believers, to whom I personally ministered. Surely, Paul could have repeated the words found in 2 Corinthians 3:1–3:

> Do we begin again to commend ourselves? Or need we, as some others, epistles of commendation to you, or letters of commendation from you? You are our epistles written in our hearts, known and read of all men: forasmuch as you are manifestly declared to be the epistle of Christ ministered by us, written not with ink, but with the Spirit of the living God; not in tables of stone, but in fleshly tables of the heart.

In the phrase "If to others I am not an apostle," the word that the apostle Paul uses is *állois*, the dative masculine plural of the adjective *állos* (243), another of the same kind. Although his apostleship is not recognized by some, he does not label them as unbelievers, in which case he would have called them *hetérois*, others, from *héteros* (2087), others of a different kind. So many times in our Christian walk, when people disagree with us or do not offer us the proper respect and acknowledgment of our labor among them, we are tempted to call them unbelievers or label them with names which are inappropriate. Not so Paul. He would have appreciated acknowledgment of his apostolicity by the Corinthians among whom he labored, but he recognized that there were those who differed with him. He did not reject them as unbelievers. He recognized that to each the Lord has given a particular task in spreading the gospel, but it is the Lord who gives the divine increase (1 Cor. 3:5–9). He calls himself and the others "laborers together with God," and he calls the believers "God's building."

It seems that the rejection he experienced by some of his brethren in Corinth was complete, as is indicated by *ouk* (3756), the absolute "not" in the phrase, "If I am not an apostle." This was an example of his humility and longsuffering. He, indeed, practiced what he wrote in 1 Corinthians 13:4, that love suffers long (*makrothumeí* [3114]), a word used to indicate one's relationship with people.

"Nevertheless to You I Am"

The expression that occurs in the next sentence, "but to you I am," is *allá* (235), but, nevertheless; *ge* (1065), a particle of emphasis meaning "and indeed" that together would translate "nevertheless indeed"; *humín* (5213), to you, the dative plural form of the second person personal pronoun, *sú* (4771), you. This is an assertive personal statement which brought great comfort to Paul. To some who did not want to acknowledge him, he may not have been considered an apostle, but to others, he was. The only other place that the expression *allá ge* occurs is in Luke 24:21. The two disciples, on the way to Emmaus, said to the risen but as yet unrecognized Lord, "But we trusted that it had been He which should have redeemed Israel: but nevertheless indeed [*allá ge*], in spite of all this, today is the third day since these things were done."

There is a lesson that we can learn from the apostle Paul. As he knew that his work among the Corinthians was resultful and effective and he rested on this fact, so we can find tremendous satisfaction and comfort knowing that our work for the Lord has not been in vain.

"For You Are the Seal of My Apostleship in the Lord"

Furthermore, the apostle, in recognition of his ministry of love among the Corinthians, says, "For you are the seal of my apostleship in the Lord." The word *sphragís* (4973), seal, is a confirmation that his work among the Corinthians was truly the work of the Holy Spirit. In fact, in Ephesians 1:13, the work of the grace of God is the one that is sealed by the Holy Spirit: "In whom you also trusted, after that you heard the word of truth, the gospel of your salvation: in whom also, having believed, you were sealed [*esphragísthēte*, the aorist passive indicative, second person plural of *sphragízō* {4972}, to seal] with that Holy Spirit of promise." (See also Eph. 4:30.)

In Romans 4:11, Paul calls the work of faith in the hearts of the believers a seal of righteousness, which was his main emphasis insofar as the believers in Corinth were concerned. He wanted the assurance that they were sealed into the body of Jesus Christ. Paul rejoiced when new believers experienced the baptism of the Holy Spirit (1 Cor. 12:13). For Paul, this was the important act, not simply the recognition by them of his apostleship.

Note that the phrase "in the Lord" has the same emphasis as in the previous verse. The work of Paul was in the Lord, it was the work of the Holy Spirit.

LESSONS:

1. In spite of his faithful labor among the Corinthians, Paul did not experience a spirit of unity among them, for there were divisions in the body. The conclusion, therefore, of his two epistles which is found in 2 Corinthians 13:11 is most appropriate: "Finally, brethren, farewell. Be perfect, be of good comfort, **be of one mind,** live in peace; and the God of love and peace shall be with you."
2. Paul did not label all those who did not recognize his apostleship as unbelievers, although he must have experienced some measure of grief for their lack of the recognition of his work in the Lord.
3. He called the believers the seal of his apostleship, which meant the certificate of the effectiveness of his work.
4. He recognized his ministry as a ministry in the Lord.
5. The word "seal" is representative of the work of faith and of the Holy Spirit.

1 Cor. 9:3 | *Paul Answers His Critics*

My own answer to them who question me is this:

Some Corinthian believers doubted the apostolicity of Paul and wondered why he chose such a rigorous life for himself in the midst of the Corinthian abundance. In the eighth chapter of 1 Corinthians, he defends his position of not banqueting in Corinth and eating the meats sacrificed to idols, although he must have found them tasty and cheap and of the best quality, but for the sake of the weak brother, he felt that he should abstain. The Corinthian Christians could not understand such conduct of depriving themselves merely for the sake of setting an example for others.

Paul chose not to marry because he believed that since marriage involved sacrificial love for one's spouse, and since husbands ought to love their wives as their own bodies (Eph. 5:28), that would take much effort and time that, as far as he was concerned, could be spent for the Lord (1 Cor. 7:33). He thus preferred to remain unmarried. In 1 Corinthians 9:5, he states that being a valid apostle should not deprive him of being married. He knew he could be chaste (1 Cor. 7:9) and be fully engaged in the Lord's work if he chose to remain unmarried, which he did, not as a matter of a command from a superior, but of conscience.

The other thing that proved him peculiar to some in Corinth was the fact that he did not want to get paid for work done. This was misunderstood as an implication that his work was unworthy of pay. He defends his position vigorously in this chapter (vv. 11–18).

"My Own Answer"

I have elected to translate the Greek word *apología* (627) as "answer," but it has come to mean a defense before a tribunal or before those who want to have an answer to a specific concern as a result of what has been said or in response to a person's actions. The verb is *apologéomai* from the preposition *apó* (575), from, and *lógos* (3056), speech, a speech that seeks to explain why a word was spoken or conduct enacted. The verb is used twice in the Gospel of Luke. The first is in 12:11 where the Lord tells His disciples not to be overanxious as to what they are to say (*apologḗsēsthe*, the aorist middle deponent subjunctive, second person plural of *apologéomai* [626], to answer back giving justification for the word spoken or action done) when they are persecuted and brought before the synagogues and authorities.

The second time that it occurs is in Luke 21:14 instructing the disciples that they should not be concerned ahead of time about what answers to give, because the Lord would be their mouth and their wisdom.

Then on six occasions the verb *apologéomai* is given in the book of Acts. When Alexander sought to explain to the confused crowd in the theater in Ephesus about who Paul was and what he was doing in their city, we read in 19:33 that "Alexander beckoned with his hand, and would have made his explanation." This is rendered by the verb *apologeísthai*, the present middle/passive deponent infinitive of *apologéomai*. Also in the book of Acts, we find the apostle Paul giving his defense before Felix

(24:10), before Festus (25:8; 26:24), and before Agrippa (26:1, 2).

Paul uses the opposite word *anapológētos* (379), defenseless, an adjective derived from the privative alpha (*a* [1]) without, and *apologéomai*, to excuse, as in Romans 1:20. It means without any acceptable answer or defense or excuse. He says, "For the invisible things of Him from the creation of the world are clearly seen." The person who looks at creation and does not see that there is a Creator behind it is without excuse. The verb in the phrase "are clearly seen" is *kathorátai*, the present passive indicative, third person singular of *kathoráō* (2529), to see clearly and visibly with one's eyes and to understand with the mind. Then we have the phrase, "being understood [*nooúmena*, the present passive participle of *noéō* {3539}, to understand] by the things that are made, even His eternal power and divinity [*theiótēs* {2305}]; so that they are without excuse [*anapologḗtous*, the accusative masculine plural of the adjective *anapológētos*]."

In Romans 2:1, the person who is criticizing another but is doing the same thing himself is told, "Therefore you are inexcusable [*anapológētos*], Oh man, whoever you are who judges: for wherein you judge another, you condemn yourself; for you who judge do the same things."

The word *apología* in the epistles, with the exception of 1 Peter 3:15, is exclusively used by the apostle Paul in 1 Corinthians 9:3; 2 Corinthians 7:11; Philippians 1:7, 17; and 2 Timothy 4:16. It is the exceptional and consecrated life of his apostolicity that Paul is really defending. In 1 Corinthians 9:3, it is as if he says, I am an apostle, and I have all the authority to enjoy life like everyone else. Nevertheless, I have made my choice in life concerning the example that I should provide; a life of celibacy, simplicity, and self-employment lest I would be accused of fulfilling my calling for the sake of money. Paul wanted to show the Corinthians that he was sincere, and the privations which he was undergoing were for the sake of the gospel (Phil. 1:7, 12). Paul, indeed, practiced what Peter says in his first epistle (1 Pet. 3:15): "But sanctify the Lord God in your hearts: and be ready always to give an answer (*apologían*) to every man that asks of you the reason of the hope that is in you, with meekness and fear." Paul gave the best example of sacrificial living, even as his Lord, and that is why he could justifiably say in 1 Corinthians 11:1, "You be imitators of me, even as I am of Christ."

Who does Paul have in mind as he gives an answer insofar as his philosophy of life as an apostle is concerned?

He says, "My own answer [*hē emḗ apología*]." Paul calls the answer he gives to the investigative criticism as his own answer and not an authoritative answer. He says *hē emḗ*, the nominative feminine singular first person possessive of the pronoun *emós* (1699), my. He intimates that it may not be your answer or anyone else's answer, but it is his answer insofar as his own life is concerned. To another Christian, this answer may not be valid. Paul is not giving the general response to sacrificial living, but his own response and reason for it. His philosophy of life was something that he personally chose.

His Hope Was for Heavenly Rewards

The basic reason for his choice is one little word—"hope" (*elpís* [1680], hope, anticipation, usually with a life of deep spiritual satisfaction in the interim). For the apostle Paul, hope was not the betterment of present living conditions. He believed that this present age was (and is) under the bondage of corruption (Rom. 8:21). In such a state in which it is, it can have no hope of improvement, but of liberation. The believers look forward to their glorious liberation. Our present body is also indicative of this slavery, and its only hope is "the redemption of our body" (Rom. 8:23). Paul, in 1 Corinthians 9:10, refers to this hope twice. The plower should plow in hope, and he that threshes in hope should be a partaker of his hope. This is the hope of the separation of that which is useless from that which is useful and promising. As we live in this world of iniquity, we experience the plowing and the threshing in our daily lives. True, Paul decided to live a life of privation. It was his privilege (*exousía* [1849], authority) to enjoy all that God had made, but he decided to go without many things which others fully enjoy. As he says in verse 22, "To the weak I became as weak that I may gain the weak: I am made [*gégona*, I have become, the perfect active indicative, first person singular of *gínomai* {1096}, I become] all things to all men, that I might by all means save some." To Paul, saving a soul, or being used by God to save a soul, was far more precious and pleasurable than having anything else in the world.

Earthly Sacrifices Are Going to Have Heavenly Rewards

Paul teaches that sacrifices for God are going to be rewarded accordingly. In this chapter of First Corinthians, he wants us to realize his own reason for such a lifestyle, and in Colossians 1:5 he says, "For the hope which is laid up for you in heaven, whereof you heard before in the word of the truth of the gospel." The more sacrifices, the greater the rewards of heaven. They are proportionate to the sacrifices on this earth.

But these sacrifices do not leave us unsatisfied in our earthly pilgrimage. There is present pleasure to be derived from such sacrifices. There is an adjective in Greek which means "each one individually" (*hékastos* [1538]). In Matthew 16:27 the Lord said, "For the Son of man shall come in the glory of his Father with the angels; and then he shall reward each man [*hekástō*, the dative masculine singular of the adjective *hékastos*, to each one] according to his works." The translation which says "to everyone" is not adequate because it gives us the idea that everyone is going to be rewarded equally, while this promised reward is varied according to one's works on earth. Works do not count for salvation, but they do count after salvation. Our lifestyle on this earth will have the special reward it deserves. "For we are his workmanship, created in Christ Jesus unto good works, which God has before ordained that we should walk in them" (Eph. 2:10). Not all Christians walk alike. As they vary in their walk, so they will vary in their rewards.

Paul realized that God gave him the grace to endure the sacrificial life he lived, and so he wanted to remain faithful to his individual calling of God. Notice the following verses where the word *hékastos* is used, but unfortunately, sometimes translated "every man," whereas it should be "to each individual man":

1 Corinthians 3:5: "Who then is Paul, and who is Apollos, but ministers by whom you believed, even as the Lord gave to each man individually [*hekástō*]."

1 Corinthians 3:8: "Now he that plants and he that waters are one: and each man [*hékastos*] shall receive his own [*ídion* {2398}, one's own, private] reward according to his own [*ídion*] labor."

1 Corinthians 3:13: "Each [*hekástou*] man's work shall be manifest: for the day shall declare it, because it shall be revealed by fire; and the fire shall try each man's [*hekástou*] work of what sort it is."

1 Corinthians 4:5: "Therefore judge nothing before the time, until the Lord come, who both will bring to light the hidden things of darkness, and will make manifest the counsels of the hearts: and then shall each man [*hekástō*, the dative masculine singular of *hékastos*] have praise of God."

And then finally, 2 Corinthians 5:10 ought to be noted: "For we must all appear before the judgment seat of Christ; that each one [*hékastos*] may receive the things done in his body, according to that he has done, whether it be good or bad."

Thus, Paul gives the reason for choosing the life that he did, not taking advantage of all his rights, but rather doing the things that would contribute to the salvation of souls, the edification of believers and the glory of God. He knew God would take care of the rewards.

"To Them Who Question Me Is This"

That Paul was criticized, there is no doubt. To whom does he give the reason for the choices that he was making in life? He says to those who investigate him for the sake of accusing him before a tribunal, "my own answer [*apología*] to those is this." The Greek text has *toís*, to those who, the dative masculine plural particle of *ho* (3588), the; *emé* (1691), me, the accusative singular first person possessive of the pronoun *egṓ* (1473), I; *anakrínousin*, who investigate, the present active participle, dative masculine plural of *anakrínō* (350), to investigate. Why were they investigating Paul? For the purpose of accusing him before a tribunal. The accusers of Paul wanted to prove him a misfit, thus making his sacrifices worthless. He was not married, and although he had every right to be married, he chose not to. He worked without charge and did not want to receive a salary for the work that he did, yet he worked harder than everyone else. He could have asked for favors, but he would not, lest he should become an offense to them. Undoubtedly, in spite of the fact that he was recognized by most as an apostle, he was criticized for having imposed upon himself such a rigorous life (1 Cor. 9:27) instead of being commended for it. Although an apostle, he considered himself no more than a servant of Christ. The word "servant" in 1 Corinthians 4:1 is *hupērétēs* (5257), an underrower, a subordinate servant who wants to accomplish the commands of his superior. "Let a man so account of us, as of the ministers of Christ [*hupērétas*] and stewards of the mysteries of God." Indeed, Paul himself was a mystery of God. How could he live the way he did when he could have enjoyed all the privileges of life which others enjoyed?

In the third verse Paul writes, "But with me it is a very small thing that I should be judged of you [*anakrithṓ,* to be investigated, the aorist passive subjunctive, first person singular of *anakrínō*] or of man's judgment: yea, I judge not my own self." Paul did not want to be judged by human criteria, but by the criteria of God. He says, "He that judges me is the Lord" (v. 4). Paul classified himself as a spiritual man (*pneumatikós* [4152]) who, according to 1 Corinthians 2:15, judges (*anakrínei*) all things, yet he himself is not judged by any man (*anakrínetai*), but by God (1 Cor. 4:4). This is the argument on which he based the sixth chapter of 1 Corinthians, that believers should not resort to unbelieving judges because their standards and principles of judging are worldly and not spiritual (1 Cor. 6:1, 6). Paul's answer was directed to those who were led by natural (*psuchikós* [5591]) principles rather than spiritual.

LESSONS:

1. Even being an apostle does not exempt one from criticism.
2. Be careful to identify the nature of criticism, who it is criticizing you, and to ask specifically about their criticism.
3. Examine yourself to see if there is any merit to the criticism.
4. Part of the answer should be connected with the particular call that God has given you. Do not think that God must give the same call to everyone.
5. Impress upon your critics that you believe that your choices in this life are made in view of one's eternal rewards in heaven.

1 Cor. 9:4 | *The Apostles' Right to Be Properly Maintained*

Do we not have the right to eat and drink?

It seems that the apostle Paul experienced some severe and unfair criticism. His response should have brought shame on the fault finders who were making life difficult for him.

"Do We Not Have the Right?"

This is a question which necessitates an affirmative answer. It starts with the particle of relative negation, *mḗ* (3361).

The second negative particle is the absolute *ou*, which, because the next word begins with a vowel, becomes *ouk* (3756), not. It goes with the verb that follows it which is *échomen*, the present active indicative, first person plural of *échō* (2192), to have. Paul is asking the question, Don't we have that which constitutes the absolute and basic right of any human being, let alone an apostle, to eat and to drink? It is as if the apostle Paul is asserting the humanity of apostleship.

Here the word *exousía* (1849), authority, right and might, is used for the first time in this chapter. It is also used in verses 4, 5, 6, 12 (twice) and 18, more here than in any other chapter. In addition, we find the word *exousía* in 1 Corinthians 8:9 where the apostle Paul gave a general principle: "But take heed lest your authority become a stumblingblock to them that are weak."

The English reader may be confused by the various translations which the word *exousía,* authority, is given in different versions of the New Testament. Whereas, for instance, in 1 Corinthians 8:9, the KJV translates the word as "liberty," and in chapter 9, verses 4, 5, 6, 12 (twice), and 18 it translates it as "power." It helps to understand that it is the same Greek word that is used, *exousía*, authority. Paul argues in defense of his philosophy of life as an apostle that he first and basically had the authority to live a normal human life, eating the necessary foods and drinking the necessary liquids to sustain himself.

"To Eat and Drink"

"To eat" is *phageín*, the aorist active infinitive of *esthíō* (2068). "To drink" is *pieín*, the aorist active infinitive of *pínō* (4095). The aorist tense implies the periodic and repetitive eating and drinking to maintain human life.

The first thing the apostle Paul declared with this statement is that an apostle is a normal human being who does not need to be an ascetic. To serve the Lord, one does not need to close himself in a monastery and deprive himself of what God has made for man's well-being and his basic maintenance. It was said of John the Baptist, who was an ascetic, that he came neither eating nor drinking, and they said, "He has a devil." But of Jesus Christ, as He walked through His earthly life in the manner of men, we find that "The Son of man came eating and drinking, and they said, 'Behold, a man gluttonous, and a winebibber, a friend of publicans and sinners' " (Matthew 11:18, 19). The Lord, by His eating and drinking, gave evidence of His humanity. But this was criticized by His contemporaries. Critics rarely analyze our motives to see why we do what we do and live the way we live.

The disciples of Jesus were not like the disciples of John the Baptist who fasted often, but they ate and drank regularly (Luke 5:33). Paul refrained from eating and drinking for a period of three days after his conversion (Acts 9:9). He said in 1 Timothy 4:4, "For every creature of God is good, and nothing to be refused, if it is received with thanksgiving." If we seek God's kingdom, God adds what is needed (Matt. 6:31–34). In 1 Corinthians 10:31 Paul says, "Whether, therefore, you eat or drink or whatever you do, do all to the glory of God." Yet Paul chose to voluntarily place restrictions on his eating and drinking if such were to become a scandal or a stumblingblock to his weaker brother (Rom. 14:21; 1 Cor. 8:7–13).

LESSONS:

1. Apostles don't have to be ascetics to prove they were apostles.
2. They are entitled to the basic provisions of life.
3. They ought to exercise voluntary restrictions in view of the weak consciences of their brethren and of unbelievers.

1 Cor. 9:5 | *Christian Workers Are Not Required to Be Celibate*

Do we not have the right to take along a sister as a wife, just as the rest of the apostles and the brothers of the Lord, and Cephas?

Whereas in the previous verse Paul referred to the basic human right to maintain himself with food and drink, here he refers to the basic privilege of marital companionship. This is the second basic right which an apostle, as a normal human being, has freedom to enjoy. The fact that Paul was an apostle did not deprive him of this privilege.

In 1 Corinthians 7 Paul also argues that marriage is a basic human right (vv. 25–35). However, he elected to remain single. Although unmarried, he maintained his purity, for he did not believe in fornication (1 Cor. 6:18). His remaining celibate, however, was not an order from Christ that he had to obey, but something that he voluntarily chose to do. As to his purity in celibacy and his philosophy of life, Paul did not hesitate to recognize that they were due to the grace of God bestowed upon him: "But by the grace of God I am what I am: and His grace which was bestowed on me was not in vain; but I labored more abundantly than they all: yet not I, but the grace of God which was with me" (1 Cor. 15:10).

"Do We Not Have the Right?"

First Corinthians 9:5 begins exactly like verse 4, "Do we not have [*mḗ* {3361}, the relative 'not'; *ouk* {3756}, the absolute 'not,' which goes with the verb *échomen* {2192}, we have] the right [*exousía* {1849}, authority, right]? . . ." The verb "have" is in the plural just like in the first instance in the previous verse, where it referred to the physical maintenance of life.

"To Take Along a Sister *as* a Wife"

"Do we not have the right to take along a sister [*adelphḗn*, the accusative feminine singular of the noun *adelphḗ* {79}, sister]," meaning a sister in the Lord, a spiritual sister. Notice that Paul does not say a woman or a wife (*gunaíka* [1135]) because not any woman could make a good wife for an apostle or a servant of the Lord, or for that matter, any born-again believer. In 1 Corinthians 7:39, Paul implies that a born-again believer ought to marry "in the Lord." How much more one who endeavors to serve the Lord! And in 2 Corinthians 6:14, he says, "Be you not unequally yoked together with unbelievers: for what fellowship has righteousness with unrighteousness? And what communion has light with darkness?" Certainly this would include the bond of marriage, for there could be no closer earthly bond that man could establish than the bond of marriage. Christ has certainly instructed us that the believer's commitment to God takes precedence in those unfortunate situations when two commitments are in conflict (Matt. 10:37; Luke 9:59–62). A Christian who is married to a non-Christian should seek to maintain the relationship, to raise any children as believers, and to win the unbelieving spouse (1 Cor. 7:12–16; 1 Pet. 3:1–12). We deduce, therefore, that the doctrine of the apostle Paul was that the wife of an apostle ought to be a sister in the Lord first of all, a believer with whom he can have spiritual communion and fellowship.

The second thing Paul said is that this woman who provides fellowship and assistance should be his wife (*gunaíka*, the accusative feminine singular of the noun *gunḗ*, woman, wife). In Luke 8:1–3, we find women who were believers who served the Lord and the apostles as they evangelized the different cities. No apostle, however, took one particular woman as a traveling companion without being joined to her as a wedded wife.

The verb that Paul uses is *periágein*, the present active infinitive of *periágō* (4013), to lead about. This comes from the preposition *perí* (4012), about, and *ágō* (71), to lead. Paul asserts his right to be married and take his wife on his journeys to execute his missionary work with him. If there was any apostle who needed the comfort and the assistance of a wife, it was certainly Paul in his many travels. Nevertheless, he preferred not to use this right but to remain single. He knew that a wife would be a great help, but he was also aware of the fact that he would be anxious about caring for her (1 Cor. 7:32–35) which, in his circumstances, would have been difficult. For him to be free to do God's work came first in his life. This is why he gives the advice to those who are not married to consider a celibate ministry (1 Cor. 7:8, 9). The verb *periágō* does not have a social significance here referring to a woman to be taken around for social functions, but rather a wife to take with him to visit the various towns and groups of his ministry, as the word is used in the Gospels (Matt. 4:23; 9:35; Mark 6:6). As Paul recounts the hardships suffered in his ministry, we can understand the added difficulty he would have had had he been married and had a family.

"Just as the Rest"

This is translated from the Greek *hoi*, the nominative masculine plural article *ho* (3588), the; *loipoí*, the nominative masculine plural of the adjective *loipós* (3062), the rest, which refers to the apostles who were married and had the privilege of being accompanied by their wives and being supported by the churches to whom they ministered. There is no doubt that the argument of the apostle Paul was that there were those apostles who clearly had these privileges of support by the churches to whom they ministered, and, while he himself was equal, he did not avail himself of the privilege. Every one of these arguments should be taken in conjunction with verse 12: "If others are recipients of this right [*exousía*, authority, right], are we not much more? Nevertheless, we did not use this right [*exousía*], but are enduring all things, so that we may not cause a hindrance to the gospel of Christ."

The privilege of being married and, as a couple, supported by the churches to whom he ministered was just as much a right and privilege for Paul as it was for the other apostles.

"Of the Apostles and the Brothers of the Lord"

The apostles and the brothers of the Lord constitute two groups of people who have the basic right to marry, and take their wives on their journeys and be supported by those to whom they minister. It does not mean that Paul is asserting that all the apostles and all the brothers of the Lord Jesus Christ were married. He asserts only that they have the right to these basic privileges of life. Therefore, it is neither necessary for us to inquire into who of the apostles were married and who were not, nor to assume that all the brothers of the Lord were married.

The brothers of the Lord Jesus were the sons of Mary and Joseph, for we read in Matthew 1:25 that Joseph "knew her not till she had brought forth her firstborn son: and he called his name Jesus." The names of Jesus' brothers are mentioned in Mark 6:3 as James, Joses, Judas, and Simon (cf. Matt. 13:55). In 1 Corinthians 15:5, the group to whom the risen Christ appeared is mentioned as "the twelve" who were commissioned to be apostles (Matt. 10:1, 2). One of these is James, the brother of the Lord (1 Cor. 15:7), to whom Jesus appeared after His resurrection. In 1 Corinthians 9:5, Paul mentions Cephas (or Peter) as the apostle who we know had a wife, since the Lord, apparently during His Galilean ministry, lived with them and healed Cephas' mother-in-law (Luke 4:38, 39).

LESSONS:

1. Paul defends his decision to remain unmarried for the purpose of serving the Lord in an unhindered way (1 Cor. 7:7, 20, 32).
2. He, as an apostle of Jesus Christ, had the same right to be married as any other apostle or a brother of the Lord.
3. Being an apostle and brother of the Lord did not deprive them of the privilege of marriage and the maintenance of their bodies.

1 Cor. 9:6

Paul and Barnabas Supported Themselves in the Lord's Work

Or is it only I and Barnabas who do not have the right of gainful employment?

When Paul came to Corinth, he was determined not to be paid for his spiritual work. He had not been commissioned and paid by a sending church or agency. In Corinth, he stayed with Aquilla and Priscilla who were tentmakers by trade (Acts 18:3). It is clear that he worked with them in their trade for the purpose of earning his living. He did not want to take money from those to whom he ministered the gospel, although he had every right to do so (1 Cor. 9:11). The reason for this was that the Corinthians were, for the most part, well-to-do and might misunderstand and accuse him of having come to Corinth to enrich himself.

How different the attitude of the Macedonians was, as described in 2 Corinthians 8:1–5! They were willing (*authaíretoi*, the nominative masculine plural of the adjective *authaíretos* [830], self-motivated, spontaneous, voluntary) to give generously out of their poverty. In the fourth chapter of 1 Corinthians, Paul chides the rich Corinthians by telling them in verses 7 and 8,

> For who makes you to differ from another? And what have you that you did not receive? Now if you did receive it, why do you glory, as if you

> have not received it? Now you are full, now you are rich, you have reigned as kings without us: and I would to God you did reign, that we also might reign with you.

In contrasting the plight of the apostles, Paul says in verse 9, "For I think that God has set forth us the apostles last, as it were appointed to death: for we are made a spectacle unto the world, and to angels, and to men." Then in verse 11 he says, "Even unto this present hour we both hunger, and thirst, and are naked, and are buffeted, and have no certain dwelling place." There is no doubt that while Paul was in Corinth as an apostle, he was wanting in his physical provisions, and because of that he wrote in verse 12, ". . . and labor, working with our own hands: being reviled, we bless; being persecuted, we suffer it." Because he did not want to take any money from the Corinthians to whom he ministered, he did manual labor to meet his physical needs. This was not because he was not entitled to support, but because he chose not to take it. Thus pointing to his own example, he writes in 1 Corinthians 10:32, 33: "Give no offense, neither to the Jews nor to the Gentiles, nor to the church of God: even as I please all men in all things, not seeking my own profit, but the profit of many, that they may be saved."

"Or Is It Only I?"

The word "only" is expressed by *mónos* (3441), meaning alone. Paul singles himself out. It is not out of pride that he implies that he may be the only one with this philosophy of life in serving the Lord, and, indeed, he does so at the risk of being misunderstood by others as being peculiar.

Paul firmly believed that the reward of each believer would be measured according to his individual commitment to the Lord and sacrifices for Him. As he reviewed the life and conduct of other apostles, and his own sacrifices enumerated in

1 Corinthians 4:8–13 and 2 Corinthians 11:22–33, he exclaimingly asked the question, "Do I alone suffer these things?" Paul believed that he was a servant (*diákonos* [1249], deacon), that is, one who was called to meet a certain need and has done so without any personal consideration or for any benefit that he may derive from it (2 Cor. 3:6; Eph. 3:7; Col. 1:23–25).

Paul also believed that God knows what each person is capable of doing and how diligently he does it according to his abilities which are divinely given (1 Cor. 4:7). God keeps a report card for each Christian as to how we utilize our talents for His glory, and this card will be used by Christ in the day of accounting (2 Cor. 5:10; Rev. 22:12).

Thus Paul writes to Timothy in 1 Timothy 3:13: "For those who ministered well [*diakonḗsantes*, the aorist active participle, nominative masculine plural of *diakonéō* {1247}, to serve in order to meet a need irrespective of any reward; *kalṓs* {2573}, an adverb meaning rightly, suitably, with propriety, becomingly] will be receiving for themselves their grade accordingly. . . ."

Paul uses two words found only in this passage in writing to his young understudy. These words have been little noticed or understood but explain why he has pursued a life of sacrifice in the ministry. The first word is *bathmós* (898), grade, derived from the verb *baínō*, to go or climb up a step or to move forward. It has rightly come to mean evaluation, rank, grade, as one would receive on his school report card. The father would ask his child, "What are the grades that you have on your report card?" As it is, the grades reveal the dedication and hard work that a child puts forth in the work he has to do, according to his age and ability. Paul recognizes that each child of God behaves individually, for he has that freedom (*exousía* [1849], authority, right) to make certain choices in his everyday life. It is only right that God grade and record, according to His standard of justice, the accomplishment of each child of His so that when the day of rewards comes, He may execute justice to each one according to his performance.

The second word that Paul uses in 1 Timothy 3:13 is the verb *peripoioúntai*, the present middle indicative, third person plural of *peripoiéō* (4046) which is used in the New Testament (TR) only twice (Acts 20:28; 1 Tim. 3:13) and is translated "purchase." It is also used in Luke 17:33 in the Nestle's Text and is translated "keep" (NASB). In reality, however, the word means to "treat oneself to the recognition of his hard work" or "to earn" a grade or recognition for his work. The verb derives from the preposition *perí* (4012) which denotes acquisition concerning work performed, and *poiéō* (4160), to make. It means to make the recognition concerning specific tasks well performed or badly performed. In the Scriptures it usually has a good connotation. This is based fundamentally on God's justice. He recognizes hard work, and He records it, and will reward it. The translation of the noun *peripoíēsis* (4047) is variably rendered as "purchased possessions" (Eph. 1:14), "obtaining" (1 Thess. 5:9; 2 Thess. 2:14), "saving" (Heb. 10:39), and "a peculiar people" which translates *laós* (2992), a people; *eis* (1519), unto, for the purpose of; *peripoíēsin*, acquisition, obtaining or earning the corresponding grade in recognition of work done (1 Pet. 2:9).

While 1 Timothy 3:13 says that those who did serve well treat themselves to a good grade (or acknowledgment) of service (*peripoioúntai*, treat themselves to), that is not all they receive. The rest of the verse says, "And great boldness in the faith which is in Christ Jesus." In other words, such people are emboldened to do great things, and God recognizes them and takes note of what they do. This was the case with the apostle Paul. With boldness he continued to sacrifice for Christ to the very last. In fact, he had the boldness to write to the Corinthians in 1 Corinthians 9:15, "For it were better for me to die, than that any man should make my glory void." Paul did not seek the recognition of men, but he did treasure the recognition and recording of his works in the report card that he would receive in heaven one day (2 Cor. 5:10).

"And Barnabas"

This is the only place in 1 Corinthians that the name of Barnabas is mentioned by Paul as having chosen to work without remuneration. It is apparent that neither Paul nor Barnabas received material benefit for their spiritual work. Although we have no evidence that Barnabas did any spiritual work among the Corinthians, the Corinthians must have known that he had volunteered his spiritual services in other places. Barnabas must have been a well-to-do man because he owned land, sold it, and brought the money to be used by the apostles in the Jerusalem church. Born on the Island of Cyprus and named Joses, he was renamed Barnabas by the apostles (Acts 4:36). Barnabas made Saul's acquaintance in the commercial city of Tarsus after his conversion. He then introduced Saul of Tarsus to the Jerusalem church (Acts 9:26, 27). The other disciples did not accept him readily, so he declared his genuineness to the apostles (Acts 9:26–30). After that, Paul remained in Tarsus, but Barnabas remained in Jerusalem until the church there was informed of the success that the gospel had in Antioch. He was commissioned to visit that city and confirm the disciples. Having sought out Paul at Tarsus, he induced him to join him in his work at Antioch. After a year of service there, the two laborers were dispatched to Jerusalem with alms for the needy Christians of Judea (Acts 11:22–30). Soon after their return to Antioch, they were set apart by the church for the special work of evangelization. Then began what is usually called the first missionary journey of Paul. In the course of this journey they visited Cyprus and the southern parts of Asia Minor, and were accompanied as far as Perga in Pamphylia by John Mark, a relative of Barnabas (Col. 4:10) whom they had brought with them from Jerusalem. Barnabas shared in the ministry of Paul. Apparently, because he was a man of means, he did not want to receive gifts from the people to whom he ministered. His philosophy of life was similar to Paul's. The difference between Paul, however, and Barnabas was that Paul earned his living with his own hands as a tentmaker, whereas Barnabas did not accept remuneration because he was financially independent. He, too, was entitled to compensation for his ministry, but he chose not to receive it, following the example of his traveling companion. How we need to learn the sufficiency and joy of enough and of doing something for the Lord without getting paid for it! In Malachi 1:10, God condemns the selfish attitude of the children of Israel by saying, "'Who is there among you who would shut the doors [of the temple] for nothing? Neither do you kindle a fire on my altar for nothing. I have no pleasure in you,' says the Lord of hosts, 'neither will I accept an offering at your hand.' " There is nothing wrong in receiving a salary for serving in the Lord's work if it is needed, but when one already has sufficient funds to meet his needs or is unwilling to do anything in Christian service unless he is paid for it, then it is wrong.

"Who Do Not Have the Right of Gainful Employment"

The Greek text says, "Do we not have the right not to work?" which is translated from *mḗ* (3361), the relative "not" since there is no absolute prohibition by the Lord against gainful employment by the servant of Christ; *ergázesthai*, the present middle/passive deponent infinitive of *ergázomai* (2038), to labor, to work for compensation. Paul claimed that the Lord did not, in any way, prohibit an apostle or a preacher from earning his own living.

In 1 Corinthians 4:12, Paul says, "And we labor, working with our own hands." "We labor" is *kopiṓmen*, the present active indicative, first person plural of *kopiáō* (2872), to be worn out and weary, to toil. "Working" is *ergazómenoi*, the present middle/passive deponent participle, nominative masculine plural of *ergázomai*, to work, the same verb as in 1 Corinthians 9:6. This leads us to believe that while Paul was in Corinth, he was working with his own hands in order to support himself at the trade of tentmaking, in which Aquilla and Priscilla were engaged (Acts 18:2, 3). Perhaps Paul was living with them. He was defending his right to work in a trade that involved working with his hands, although he could have been supported by the believers in Corinth who benefited from his spiritual work. Everyone is entitled to choose a trade whereby he can make a living.

Greek and Roman mentality regarded those who lived by labor as being indispensable, but nevertheless contemptible necessities. Jewish teaching, however, stood in strong contrast to this, and laborious work was accepted as a rule of life. Even the scholar was to spend some of his time in manual work. Paul, in his teaching, emphasizes this. He writes in 2 Thessalonians 3:10, "If any man would not work, neither should he eat." A man who does no work is, to the church, a parasite. In the Thessalonian church, the expectation of the Second Coming of the Lord had been made an excuse by many for the abandonment of their daily work. Paul reminds his converts how, when he had preached to them, he had taught them to welcome a life of labor. It brings with it three good effects—quietness of spirit, honorable standing among neighbors, and independence of other men's alms (1 Thess. 4:11, 12; 2 Thess. 3:12). To these he adds, in Ephesians 4:28, the ability to help those who are in need. That he might be no burden to others, he willingly worked overtime day and night, as he says in 1 Thessalonians 2:9 and 2 Thessalonians 3:8. His roughened hands showed the severity of his toil (Acts 20:33–35). Having unselfishly chosen this manual labor, however, Paul became the target of attacks depreciating him for his labor, and claiming that his manual labor proved that he was not worthy of support as an apostle. Consequently, he defends his right to work like anyone else for a living. This was because he, himself, made the choice not to be compensated for spiritual work that he performed among the Corinthians. He did not wish material compensation for his spiritual work, especially among the Corinthians, neither because he did not have the right nor was he unworthy of it, but because of his own choice of principle and conscience (vv. 11, 12).

LESSONS:

1. Paul does not hesitate to isolate himself as an exception to the general rule of compensation for labor performed.
2. He labored with his own hands by being a tentmaker, along with Priscilla and Aquilla, his companions in Corinth.
3. He did not allow his trade to overwhelm him in the use of his time, but he balanced it all so that he could make a living and, at the same time, preach the gospel.
4. He also recalled the example of Barnabas, who probably was well-to-do and neither needed to labor, nor accepted compensation for his spiritual work.
5. He would not allow the Corinthians to consider his apostolic work as being unworthy of compensation because he chose not to receive it.
6. He defends the choice he made to do manual work and, at the same time, preach the gospel. This was his inalienable right which no one had the authority to condemn.

1 Cor. 9:7 — The Principle of Compensation

Who at any time serves as a soldier at his own expense? Who plants a vineyard and does not eat of its fruit? Or who tends a flock and does not feed on the milk of the flock?

Paul now poses three questions to which a negative answer is anticipated.

"Who at Anytime Serves as a Soldier at His Own Expense?"

"Who [*tís* {5101}, the nominative masculine singular interrogative pronoun] serves as a soldier [*strateúetai*, the present middle indicative, third person singular of *strateúō* {4754}, to enlist to serve as a soldier] at his own [*idíois*, the dative masculine plural of the adjective *ídios* {2398}, one's own, individual or private] expense [*opsōníois*, the dative neuter plural of the noun *opsōnion* {3800}, whatever is bought to be eaten with bread, meaning provisions or supplies]?" The phrase "at any time" that we inserted in our translation before the verb "serves" occurs lastly in this sentence and is *poté* (4218). Nobody "at any time" is expected to buy his own food and clothing and other supplies needed to perform his duty as a soldier. These are provided for him. Paul often allegorizes the service of the Lord as being that of a soldier (2 Tim. 2:3, 4).

"Who Plants a Vineyard and Does Not Eat of Its Fruit?"

The second illustration that Paul presents is that of a farmer. "Who plants a vineyard [*tís*, who; *phuteúei*, the present active indicative, third person singular of *phuteúō*, {5452} to plant; *ampelṓna*, the accusative masculine singular of the noun *ampelṓn* {290}, a vineyard] and does not eat of its fruit [*kaí* {2532}, and; *ek* {1537}, from, out of; *karpoú*, the genitive masculine singular of the noun *karpós* {2590}, fruit; *autoú*, the genitive masculine singular personal of the pronoun *autós* {846}, he, himself; *ouk* {3756}, the absolute 'not'; *esthíei*, the present active indicative, third person singular of *esthíō* {2068}, to eat] of its fruit?"

In 2 Timothy 2:6 the apostle says, "The husbandman [*geōrgón*, the accusative masculine singular of the noun *geōrgós* {1092}, farmer] that labors must be first partaker of the fruits."

"Or Who Tends a Flock and Does Not Feed on the Milk of the Flock"

The third allegory is that of a shepherd. The verb "tends" is translated from *poimaínei*, the present active indicative, third person singular of *poimaínō* (4165), to shepherd, to tend a flock (*poímnēn*, the accusative singular of *poímnē* [4167], flock). The word "feed" is translated from *esthíei*, the present active indicative, third person singular of *esthíō*, to eat or "feed on" because milk is a liquid and has great nourishing qualities.

As it is natural for the soldier to be supplied with his upkeep and for the farmer to eat grapes from the vineyard in which he labors (cf. Deut. 20:6; Prov. 27:18) and for the shepherd to feed on the milk of the flock he tends, it is perfectly legitimate and natural for the servant of Christ to be a partaker in the work in which he engages.

The Lord Is a Just Paymaster

Paul believed that a worker was "worthy of his hire" (1 Tim. 5:18). This is a term that the Lord used when He appointed the seventy to go to the cities He was going to visit. In Luke 10:7, the Lord said, "And in the same house remain, eating and drinking such things as they give: for the laborer is worthy of his hire. Go not from house to house." The word "hire" is a translation of the Greek word *misthós* (3408) which has a variety of meanings (Matt. 20:8; Luke 10:7). One is a reward or pay to be received (Matt. 5:12, 46; 6:1, 2, 5, 16; 10:41, 42; 1 Cor. 3:14; 9:17, 18; 2 John 1:8), or it can also mean retribution or punishment (2 Pet. 2:13).

The expectation and receipt of wages for service rendered is clearly taught by the Lord in the parable of the laborers (Matt. 20:1–16) where we find two types of laborers. The first type was promised a specific wage for a specific service (v. 2). The next type included four groups who were definitely promised that they were going to receive "whatever is right," which, however, was not specified. When the end came and they received their pay, those who went to the field, trusting the lord of the vineyard to give them that which was right, were pleasantly surprised to receive greater than the amount specified to the first group. The apostle Paul placed himself in the category of those who believed in the mercifulness and justice of the One who sent him, although he did not deny the fact that the proper and natural way of working is to do so with the expectation of a commensurate reward for labor.

It is worthwhile to notice the question that the master gave as an answer to the first group of laborers who went on the promise of a definite wage for a definite service. Their master said in Matthew 20:15, "Is it not permissible [*éxesti*, it is permissible, the same word that the apostle Paul uses in 1 Cor. 6:12; 10:23, and from which the noun *exousía* {1849}, authority or right, is derived] for me to do what I will with my own?"

By this parable, our Lord is saying, I will accept your service which is restricted; I will give you the recompense as per agreement; but I am more pleased with those who are characterized by unrestricted acceptance to My call of duty. When you have done a job well and leave the reward to Me, you will get much more than you could ask or think.

In other words, the philosophy of our Lord is that if there is a job to be done in the kingdom of God and you are called to do it, do it with all your heart and without restrictions. Then when it comes to the reward, the Lord will invariably do more than if there had been a monetary agreement. In Matthew 20:13, the lord of the laborers responded to the workers who complained that he showed partiality to the ones who worked less by teaching them that his generosity should not be misunderstood and interpreted as injustice. Rather, it is freedom to do what he pleases with what is his own. It is as if Christ were saying, When it comes to service, you apply limitations on your work for Me, but when it comes to reward, I do not apply any restrictions.

Similar to this parable is the parable of faith and duty that we find in Luke 17:5–10. A bond slave (*doúlos* [1401]) can never say to his master, I have done that which I have been commanded to do and I will not do anymore (v. 10). We are unprofitable bond slaves (*doúloi*) of Christ if we ever say while engaged in His service, "We have done that which was our duty to do and will do no more."

Paul's philosophy was that he would do all that was needed to be done, as he teaches in 2 Corinthians 3:8, "This is a ministry of the Spirit in glory." What is the "ministry of the Spirit in glory [*en* {1722}, in; *dóxē* {1391}, glory, derived from *dokéō* {1380}, to recognize]"? It is that particular ministry to which each one is led by God's Spirit, the future significance and reward of which is yet to be revealed. If we truly realized that we are serving the Lord in the Holy Spirit, we would not think of placing any restrictions upon our service (*diakonía* [1248]) for accomplishing what is needed, not merely what we are paid for according to human expectations. In other words, the servant of Christ ought to realize that God is not merely a human employer who is expected to meet the minimum standards of human criteria when it comes to the reward of service for Him. It is His prerogative to determine the reward, and when He apportions it, He does it with a shovel and not with a spoon. We tend to ration our service to Him with selfish limitations. Yes, indeed, Paul acknowledges the natural and acceptable standard of the soldier who serves in the army, the farmer who labors and plants and harvests, and the shepherd who tends to sheep. The standard, however, of the bondslave of Christ is different. He does what needs to be done with joy and eagerness because he loves the Lord and leaves the reward up to Him. It is far better to depend on the mercy and the overabundance that God has at His disposal and His authority (*exousía*) than for us to depend on what any man could promise or supply (Gen. 18:25; 2 Tim. 4:8). We must, therefore, expend faithful and unrestricted service to our Lord and leave the rewards to His mercifulness.

LESSONS:

1. Compensation is the normal plan of work and reward.
2. Paul uses the illustration of a soldier expecting to receive adequate provisions when he enlists and serves in the army. He is not expected to provide for himself. As one enlists in the army of Christ, he is expected to serve and will be compensated accordingly for his work so that it will not be inhibited.

3. The farmer labors under the expectation that what he plants will grow and yield its fruit. He is to partake of that fruit, which will benefit others as well (Luke 12:13–21).
4. The shepherd who tends to his sheep partakes of the milk that the sheep produce, but not selfishly and exclusively.
5. There is a definitive interaction between planting and reaping, both on earth and in heaven. It is to be remembered that the born-again believer belongs to two kingdoms: that of earth, which is physical, and that of heaven, which is spiritual (Matt. 6:19–21).

1 Cor. 9:8 | *Man's Logic and God's Law*

Or do I speak only as a man? But does not the law say the same thing?

In verse 7, Paul spoke of the natural expectation of compensation for work. He used illustrations of the soldier, the farmer, and the shepherd. Each expected to be rewarded by the employers they served. This is the natural process of life, as man sees it.

"Or Do I Speak *Only* as a Man?"

The question that Paul now asks necessitates a negative answer: "Do I speak these things **only** as a man?" The question is asked by the use of the relative "not" (*mḗ* [3361]) as in the previous questions asked in verses 4 and 5: "Do we not have authority to eat and drink? And do we not have authority to take along a sister as a wife, as the rest of the apostles and brothers of the Lord and Cephas?" Here, having stated the normal expectation that work will be compensated, he asks, "Am I speaking these things only as a man?" In other words, Paul stresses that this principle of work and compensation is generally accepted by all men. The phraseology *katá* (2596), according to; *ánthrōpon*, the accusative masculine singular of the noun *ánthrōpos* (444), man, thus means according to man or by human principles.

This expression "according to man" is used in Romans 3:5 where Paul argues that the demonstration of the wrath of God is only considered to be unrighteousness in man's opinion which is a perverted opinion. The truth is that God brings His wrath upon those who deserve it, and they must be punished if He is to be proven righteous.

The second occurrence of the expression "according to man" is found in 1 Corinthians 3:3, where Paul claims that dissensions and quarrels come from man's worldly behavior—a behavior motivated by his own standards which are fleshly in nature, selfish, and self-seeking.

The third occurrence is here in 1 Corinthians 9:7, 8 where, using the illustrations of the soldier, the farmer, and the shepherd, Paul is speaking according to the principles of man.

The fourth occurrence is in 1 Corinthians 15:32, where Paul says, "If after the manner of men I have fought with beasts at Ephesus, of what advantage is it to me if the dead rise not?" In other words, he says, Why did I risk my life if the dead do not rise?

It occurs also in Galatians 1:11 to indicate that the gospel that Paul preached is not according to man's philosophy (see also Gal. 3:15).

The verb that Paul uses to express that he speaks according to man is *lalṓ*, the present active indicative, first person singular contracted from *laléō* (2980), to talk. It is used with the specific meaning of breaking the silence regarding the total argument as to an apostle's compensation for his work.

"But Does Not the Law Say the Same Thing?"

When, on the other hand, Paul refers to what the law says as being reasonable, he uses the verb *légei,* the present active indicative, third person singular of *légō* (3004), to say. The answer to this question is an affirmative "yes," this is what the law says, and for a reason. The one who works should have hope of a reward. God, in His law, sets the standard for this human custom. The Lord Jesus Christ, however, teaches us to go even further.

The person who loves and serves the Lord does not find his satisfaction only in material things, but in spiritual blessings and rewards.

LESSONS:

1. Paul resorts to human wisdom while saying that the soldier ought to be paid, the farmer ought to be allowed to eat of the grapes that he plants, and the shepherd ought to be able to feed upon the milk of the sheep he tends. This is part of human wisdom.
2. Living only according to human standards brings confusion and quarrels.
3. Only Christ can satisfy.

1 Cor. 9:9 — *The Law of Moses Concerning Working Animals*

For in the law of Moses it has been written, 'You must not muzzle an ox while it is threshing the corn.' Is it about the oxen only that God is concerned?

Now Paul turns from the accepted human custom of a laborer being paid for his services to the Law of Moses.

"For in the Law of Moses It Has Been Written"

In Deuteronomy 25:4 it says, "You shall not muzzle the ox when he treads out the corn." The translation "it has been written" comes from one Greek word, *gégraptai*, the perfect passive indicative, third person singular of *gráphō* (1125), to write. The perfect tense refers to what God wrote and that it is still valid (cf. 1 Cor. 1:31; 2:9; 2 Cor. 8:15; 9:9). But "the law," Paul says in Galatians 3:24, "was our schoolmaster to lead us to Christ." Now that we are in Christ, we must act accordingly and live not merely according to the law, but for Him who is the fulfillment of the law (Matt. 5:17).

"You Must Not Muzzle an Ox While It Is Threshing the Corn"

There is a definite prohibition in the use of the words *ou* (3756), the absolute "not," and *phimṓseis*, the future active indicative, second person singular of *phimóō* (5392), to muzzle. In the two instances that this expression is used (1 Cor. 9:9; 1 Tim. 5:18), it is used in connection with putting a muzzle over the mouth of an ox that threshes the corn in order to hinder the ox from eating the corn. This illustrates the argument that compensation should be given for work performed. Even as the ox is permitted to eat of the corn, so should the worker be compensated. This, Paul argues, is in accordance with human wisdom and with divine provision in the law.

"Is It About the Oxen Only That God Is Concerned?"

Then Paul asks the logical question: "Is it in only the oxen that God is interested [*mélei* {3199}, the present active indicative, third person singular of *mélō*, care, show concern {cf. Matt. 22:16; Acts 18:17}]?" The idea is to express the interest of God, not just in animals, but in the people whom the animals serve, for they can produce better work if they are well fed.

This also demonstrates the great mercy of God even upon animals. It is cruel to allow an animal to be surrounded by food, perhaps hungry, and yet be deprived of it. One of the few satisfactions an animal can have is that of a full stomach. If God cares even for dumb beasts, how much more does He care for man who is made in His image and with whom He desires to have fellowship?

<u>LESSONS</u>:

1. The idea of compensation for corresponding work was so fundamental that the Lord included it in His law that He gave through Moses. Compensation for corresponding work is not only of human sense, but also of divine law.
2. God is so merciful that His loving concern extends even to animals.

1 Cor. 9:10 | God Cares More about Mankind Than about Animals

Or is it entirely for our benefit He says this? For our sakes this was written, "The plowman is dutybound to plow in hope of reward, and the thresher shares in the hope of the plowman's hope."

Paul continues his argument stressing God's love and concern for mankind. What a dreadful world this would be if we had no hope of reward for our work. The primary interest of God, Paul teaches, is for human beings.

"Or Is It Entirely for Our Benefit He Says This?"

"Us" is *hēmás* (2248), the accusative plural of the personal pronoun *egṓ* (1473), I. "For us" is translated *di'hēmás* (1223), meaning "for our benefit." *Di'* is actually *diá* contracted by the *a* being dropped and replaced by an apostrophe because the next word starts with a vowel. In the previous verse, Paul discussed the ox, a working animal that is used to plow the ground for planting the corn, and for threshing. The ox is driven by the plowman. To refuse to allow the animal to eat what it helps to produce is counterproductive for man. Then comes the threshing process. The thresher and the plower partake of the same hope that each will benefit by the final product. God's concern, this verse emphasizes, is not for the ox alone, but for man who needs the animals to do his work. I have translated the Greek adverb *pántōs* with the meaning of entirely, certainly, assuredly (cf. Luke 4:23; Acts 18:21; 21:22; 28:4; 1 Cor. 9:22). The law teaches that man should not be cruel and inconsiderate of the animals that help to provide the very food a person eats.

The verb in the statement "For our benefit . . . He says" is *légei*, the present indicative of *légō* (3004), to say for a reason. That reason is that the more satisfied and strong the animal is, the more work he will produce. And, naturally, this work is for the benefit of man.

"For Our Sakes This Was Written"

Paul reminds us that the quotation of the Old Testament was written for us, *di'hēmás*, "for our sakes." There is a lesson for us to learn, for, "All Scripture is given by inspiration of God, and is profitable for doctrine, for reproof, for correction, for instruction in righteousness" (2 Tim. 3:16). God has instituted the concept that work must be compensated accordingly.

"The Plowman Is Dutybound to Plow in the Hope of Reward, and the Thresher Shares in the Hope of the Plowman's Hope"

Take away the hope of compensation, and the natural incentive to work also is taken away. That is the meaning of the expression *ep' elpídi* (*epí* [1909], upon, with the *i* becoming an apostrophe in front of the word *elpídi; elpís* [1680], hope, in hope of). This word "hope" is mentioned three times in this verse and it indicates the anticipation of the plowman and the reason for plowing (*arotrióō* [722], to plow), and that of the thresher (*aloáō* [248], to tread out corn, to force corn from husks by treading). The one doing the work ought to partake of the corn he threshes.

Anticipation, or hope, of partaking of one's work is certainly an incentive. The instinct of self-preservation is God-given and to be honored as such in our employing others to accomplish things. Hope of compensation must be the motivation that ought not be denied those working for us, as it is not denied to us as we work for others. This is the natural process sanctioned by divine law, for "the laborer is worthy of his hire" (Luke 10:7).

LESSONS:

1. All work must have a goal and be fruitful.
2. God meant that even the animal who is put to work ought to be compensated by being allowed to eat of the product of its labor.
3. If even the animal is to receive such considerate treatment, how much more the man who works for us?

1 Cor. 9:11 | *Spiritual Work Compensated Materially*

Since it is we, ourselves, who sowed the spiritual blessings among you, is it anything great that of you we shall reap material blessings?

The expected answer to the question posed in this verse is an emphatic "no."

"Since It Is We, Ourselves"

Paul begins this verse with the suppositional conjunction *ei* (1487), if, which may present either a mere subjective hypothesis of impossibility or introduce a condition of actuality and certainty. Because it refers to Paul's effective spiritual work among the Corinthians, we have translated this conjunction as "since." There is no doubt that Paul sowed spiritual truth among the Corinthians.

"Who Sowed Spiritual Blessings Among You"

Paul refers to his labor among them as sowing "the spiritual blessings" or "things," with the noun "blessings" or "things" implied. That makes the article in agreement with *sarkiká*, the accusative neuter plural of the adjective *sarkikós* (4559), those things pertaining to the flesh or to material living. The word *sárx* (4561), flesh, here does not have a bad moral connotation (Rom. 7:5), but is equivalent to *biōtiká* (982), material things pertaining to the means of living insofar as maintaining the body is concerned (Luke 21:34; 1 Cor. 6:3, 4). Paul contributed a great deal to the spiritual life of the Corinthian Christians, and now he argues that it is not a great thing for them to communicate something material for himself and others who sowed the spiritual seed among them. He implies the enormity of the spiritual contribution he made versus the material benefit he may receive, which would be of far less value. In introducing his work among the Corinthians, Paul writes in 1 Corinthians 1:4–9:

> I thank my God always on your behalf, for the grace of God which is given you by Jesus Christ; that in everything you are enriched by Him, in all utterance, and in all knowledge [these were the spiritual blessings Paul sowed among the Corinthians] even as the testimony of Christ was confirmed in you: so that you come behind in no gift; waiting for the coming of our Lord Jesus Christ: Who shall also confirm you unto the end, that you may be blameless in the day of our Lord Jesus Christ. God is faithful, by whom you were called unto the fellowship of His Son, Jesus Christ our Lord.

In verse 5, Paul tells the Corinthians that they were enriched (*eploutísthēte* which is the passive indicative of the verb *ploutízō* [4148], to make rich) by Jesus Christ whose grace they received as a result of his preaching among them. It is also to be noted that he reminds them that "they came behind in no gift," referring to spiritual gifts. Furthermore, the apostle Paul encouraged the Corinthian Christians in the full expectation of the coming of the Lord, which is one of the greatest spiritual blessings that can come to anyone. He taught them to live not only for the present, but also for future blessings which are eternal (2 Cor. 4:18).

Tá pneumatiká is a plural adjective of "the spiritual ones," the noun being understood as being blessings or things. In Ephesians 1:3, Paul writes, "Blessed be the God and Father of our Lord

Jesus, who has blessed us with all spiritual blessings in heavenly places in Christ." The preaching of the gospel which Paul sowed among the Corinthians brought spiritual blessings. The verb "blessed" is *eulogḗsas*, the aorist active participle, nominative masculine singular of *eulogéō* (2127), bless, which, in turn is derived from *eu* (2095), well, and *logéō*, or in its basic form, *légō* (3004), to say, speak. The verb *eulogéō*, therefore, means to speak well of, and God's Word is God's action or intervention in the lives of believers. He causes all things to work together for good in the lives of believers. The noun "blessing" is *eulogía* (2129), well-speaking of or action which results in benevolence. This is why I have elected to translate the implied noun after the adjective "the spiritual" as "blessings."

"Is It Anything Great That of You We Shall Reap Material Blessings?"

In Romans, we find the apostle Paul telling the believers who, for the most part, were Jewish converts, that he is going to see them on his way to Spain. He would bring them a contribution from the Christians of Macedonia and Achaia. These were Gentiles who were pleased to send a contribution to the Jews of Jerusalem, for they felt that they were their debtors in that they heard the gospel from them. They had participated in their spiritual blessings and were expressing their gratitude not only in the spiritual things, but also by material contributions. Paul writes in Romans 15:27, "For since [*ei* with the meaning of 'since' {cf. Matt. 6:30; 7:11; Luke 11:13; 12:28; John 7:23; 10:35; 13:14, 17, 32; Acts 4:9; 11:17; Rom. 6:8; 15:27; Col. 2:20; Heb. 7:15; 1 Pet. 1:17; 1 John 4:11}] the Gentiles have been made partakers of their spiritual *blessings* [*toís pneumatikoís*, the dative neuter plural article of *ho* {3588}, meaning 'in the'; *pneumatikoís*, spiritual, the dative neuter plural of the adjective *pneumatikós*

{4152} with the noun 'blessings' implied], their duty is also to minister unto them in material *things*." The noun is implied, which in the KJV, is translated as "things," and in the RSV and NIV is translated "blessings." Since the Jewish Christians shared their spiritual blessings with the Gentiles, the Gentile believers had a duty (*opheílousi*, the present active indicative, third person plural of *opheílō* [3784], to owe, be indebted) also to minister to them in material ways. In other words, Paul seems to express his great satisfaction that the believers of Macedonia and Achaia, who for the most part were Gentiles, did not say a mere thanks to the Jews for having proclaimed the gospel to them, but they showed their gratitude in material ways by sending a contribution. The material things with which the Gentiles were helping the Jerusalem saints is *sarkikoís*, the dative masculine plural of the adjective *sarkikós*, which means pertaining to the flesh or material things.

We find the same expression used in this verse in 1 Corinthians 9:11 where we find *sarkiká*, the accusative neuter plural of the adjective *sarkikós*. Paul definitely defends his work as being a spiritual ministry which should be recompensed materially. He who works for the spiritual benefit of others may be legitimately compensated for his time and effort. It is not that the recipient can ever pay for spiritual blessings received, but he must substantiate his heart-felt gratitude with pocket gratitude. The generosity of the purse expresses the heart's sincerity.

LESSONS:

1. A spiritual ministry ought to be considered worthy of compensation.
2. The compensation ought to include the provision of physical sustenance.
3. The words Christ spoke in Matthew 10:8, "Freely you have received, freely give," may be misunderstood to mean that he who serves Christ must do it freely. Christ, however, further elucidates in verse 10 when He says, "For the workman is worthy of his meat." What He meant by

the first statement was that spiritual services ought not to be sold for material gain, as, for instance, the selling of indulgences or the assurance of other spiritual benefits which could be bought for money (Acts 8:14–25).

4. It is good that we express our appreciation of spiritual benefits with material blessings.

1 Cor. 9:12 | *Paul Defends a Right He Personally Did Not Use*

Since others share in that which I rightfully expect of you, should we not more so? Nevertheless, we never availed ourselves of this right, but we endure all things in order that we may not cause any sudden interruption in the gospel of Christ.

Paul continues to elaborate on the right of spiritual workers to be supported by those to whom they minister, although he earned his own support by manual labor. It seems the Corinthians criticized either method the servant of God chose.

"Since Others Share"

This verse begins with the suppositional conjunction *ei* (1487), since or if. In this instance of affirmation of the right to be compensated for spiritual work in a material way, it is better if it is not translated as a conjunction of subjective doubt, "if," but rather as a conjunction of practical reality, "since" (cf. Matt. 19:10; Acts 5:39; Rom. 8:25; 1 Cor. 9:17).

Who were the others who are said to have used the right of compensation for spiritual work done? The Greek work is *álloi*, the nominative masculine plural of the adjective *állos* (243) which means others of the same kind. These were teachers and workers who were imparting spiritual blessings just as Paul was. This word probably refers to the teachers who were a blessing to the Gentile Corinthians, among whom were Jewish believers also.

The verb in Greek is *metéchousin,* to have a share, the present active indicative, third person plural of *metéchō* (3348), to have together with others. It is derived from the preposition *metá* (3326), with, denoting association, and the verb *échō* (2192), to have. This verb is used by the apostle Paul not only in this verse, but also in verse 10 and 1 Corinthians 10:17, 21, 30. The only other occurrences are in Hebrews 2:14; 5:13; 7:13. As used in 1 Corinthians 9:12, it teaches that the worker is entitled to all the benefits of his work, but that he is to share that benefit with the one who provides the work. The worker is compensated by the employer, but the employer benefits by the work done by the employee, too. Furthermore, it would indicate that others who are working together so that a certain result may come from common work are all entitled to their share of compensation. The individual worker should not begrudge that portion which the boss receives since he has provided the opportunity to earn an income.

Other Christian workers in Corinth did not follow the example of Paul by doing spiritual work among them without receiving material compensation. They did as Paul said—the worker is worthy of his pay; but not as he did—accepting no compensation at all. While in Corinth, Paul preferred to earn his living as a tentmaker in the business which Aquilla and Priscilla had (Acts 18:2, 3), but he did not consider those who were paid for their ministry as being inferior in any way.

"In That Which I Rightfully Expect of You"

And of what did Paul have the right to share? It was material compensation which the Corinthians were obligated to provide for them. The Greek text says *tḗs exousías*, the genitive of *exousía* (1849), authority, privilege, right and might. Paul uses this word in this chapter (vv. 4–6, 12 [twice], 18) more than in any other chapter of his writings.

He leaves no doubt at all that, as an apostle, he had the right to expect to be paid for his spiritual work among the Corinthians, but he did not use that right. However, he did not criticize those who did, who, nevertheless, were not even apostles. Compensation for work done is the right not only of apostles, but of anyone who serves the Lord.

"Should We Not More So?"

Then Paul asks the question, "How much more we?" In the Greek text, there is the absolute negative *ou* (3756), "not," followed by *mâllon* (3123), the comparative adverb meaning "more," and *hēmeís* (2249), we.

If others, whoever these may be, partook of the authority or privilege which we as apostles have in regard to you, how much more we who are apostles? The contrast here is between "others" and "us," meaning the apostles. Paul uses the plural "we" because he is not willing to single out himself as the only one among the apostles who is willing to sacrifice the rights of his apostleship. He implies that there were other self-sacrificing apostles, but he specifically includes himself having proven the disposition of his heart to the Corinthians.

Paul had two companions on his second missionary journey into the cities of Philippi, Thessalonica, Berea, Athens, and Corinth. Soon after the rupture of the relationship between Paul and Barnabas, Paul selected Silas as his new associate and began this journey (Acts 15:22–41). Timothy, whom Paul found at Lystra and whom he commissioned as an evangelist (Acts 16:3; 2 Tim. 1:6, 7), was sent by Paul to Corinth to remind them of his preaching and character (1 Cor. 4:17). These co-laborers of Paul may or may not have received compensation for their spiritual work among the Corinthians or others to whom they ministered. Paul, however, defends their right of compensation for such work. The decision that he made not to receive compensation was absolutely his own, but in his humility he included others who may have served the Lord with the same motive. For this reason, he uses the plural in saying, "Should not **we** more so?" It is good not to boast of one's sacrifices for Christ as if he were the only one doing so. Only the Lord knows the heart of another.

"Nevertheless, We Never Availed Ourselves of This Right"

Once again Paul uses the absolute negative *ou* with the verb *echrēsámetha*, the aorist middle deponent indicative, first person plural of *chráomai* (5530), to use, to avail. He was free to make use of this entitlement, that is to receive remuneration for the spiritual work he did among the Corinthians, but he did not avail himself of this right or privilege which he stresses by the word *exousía* (authority, right).

"But We Endure All Things in Order That We May Not Cause Any Sudden Interruption in the Gospel of Christ"

Paul further explains why he has refused this privilege. He did not simply give up conveniences that he would have enjoyed had he received compensation, "But we **endure** all things in order that we may not cause any sudden interruption in the gospel of Christ."

In 2 Corinthians 11:7, Paul wrote, "Have I committed an offense in abasing myself in that you might be exalted, because I have preached to you the gospel of God freely [without charge]?" The question which Paul poses to the Corinthians is, Did I preach to you without charging for my labor because I wasn't worthy of it, or was there another motive which stimulated me not to charge? Paul singled out the Corinthians because of their implied suspicious attitude and critical spirit. Although Paul had physical needs, he preferred not to be paid by the Corinthians and then suffer the criticism that he was preaching for the sake of money. In 2 Corinthians 11:8 he wrote, "I robbed other churches, taking wages of them, to do you service." He had in mind the generous and humble Macedonians (2 Cor. 8:1–5). He equated receiving money from them as robbing them so that he could preach the gospel to the Corinthians. Paul was careful not to give the impression that he ministered for the sake of money. His attitude ought to cause us to examine our own attitude in giving, lest we make it uncomfortable for the recipients to accept our gifts. It is to be noted that what is translated as "wages" in this verse is not the regular word *misthós* (3408) which would ordinarily be translated as compensation or wages. The word in the Greek text is *opsṓnion* (3800). This primarily signifies that which is bought to be eaten with bread, such as provisions or supplies for a soldier (Luke 3:16; 1 Cor. 9:7). This metaphorically means that which is essential for the maintenance of life and nothing extra. The Greek word for "service" in this verse is *diakonía* (1248) which implies that which one has need of, meaning the gospel of Jesus Christ. This was the desperate need of the Corinthians, and in order for Paul to meet that need in the eighteen months that he lived among them, it was necessary for him to be remembered by the poor Macedonians. It seems that working with his hands as a tentmaker was not sufficient to meet his meager needs.

Note further that 2 Corinthians 11:9 says: "And when I was present with you and wanted. . . ." The Greek word for "wanted" is *husterētheís*, the aorist passive participle, nominative masculine singular of *husteréō* (5302), to fall short, be destitute. Our admiration for Paul is that he lived in the midst of people who abundantly enjoyed the material things of life while he was in need of essentials, and yet he would not take money from them to meet those needs. And then in this same verse, he makes a statement that is absolute. The KJV translates it, "I was chargeable to no man." The NIV has, "I have kept myself from being a burden to you in any way." The Greek says *ou*, the absolute "not"; *katenárkēsa*, the aorist active indicative, first person singular of *katanarkáō* (2655), to be burdensome, derived from *katá* (2596), against, and *narkáō*, to make numb. *Nárkē*, which is the noun derived from the verb, means stiffness, numbness, a weight that causes one to sink, hence the name in Modern Greek is used for a torpedo. It is also the root word for "narcotic" in English which is something that numbs a person or puts him to sleep. It makes one insensitive to the real world around him. The word may have been used in Paul's native Tarsus in the medical school that existed there. The verb, therefore, means to render someone useless for the purpose of destroying him. As we would say in modern English, I did not drug anyone.

The last word in this sentence is *oudenós*, the genitive masculine singular of the adjective *oudeís* (3762), the absolute "nobody." Paul is saying that he did not allow himself to be a burden to a single soul and thus become a dead weight which had to be borne. This is some statement to make to a people among whom Paul lived and worked a year and a half. The verse continues: "For that which was lacking to me the brethren which came from Macedonia supplied: and in all things I have kept myself from being burdensome unto you, and so will I keep myself." In spite of the fact that Paul worked with his own hands at the tentmaking trade with Priscilla and Aquilla while he was in Corinth, what he made in the trade was not sufficient to meet his needs as he preached the gospel among the Corinthians. The lack he experienced in this ministry was met by the Macedonian Christians in spite of their poverty. Perhaps Silas and

Timothy brought these gifts to him (Acts 18:5) and at the same time preached the gospel there with him (2 Cor. 1:19). Thus Paul accepted nothing from the Corinthians while he ministered to them, nor did he accept anything from the Philippians while he was in Philippi nor from the Thessalonians while he was in Thessalonica. In writing to them in 1 Thessalonians 2:9, he says, "For you remember, brethren, our labor and travail: for laboring night and day, because we would not be chargeable [*epibarḗsai,* the aorist active infinitive of *epibaréō* {1912}, to become a burden] unto any of you, we preached unto you the gospel of God." And in 2 Thessalonians 3:8 he writes, "Neither did we eat any man's bread for naught; but wrought with labor and travail night and day, that we might not be chargeable [*epibarḗsai*] to any of you."

"But We Endure All Things"

The only reason Paul did not receive money from the Corinthians while he was at Corinth, the Philippians while he was at Philippi, and the Thessalonians while he was in Thessalonica, was to avoid any misunderstanding as to the motive of his preaching. He further states, "But we endure all things in order that we may not cause any sudden interference to the gospel of Christ." What is translated "endure" is *stégomen*, the present active indicative, first person plural of *stégō* (4722) which literally means to provide a roof over (*stégē* [4721]). Paul could have used the word *hupoménomen* (5278), to endure, in which case he would have implied that the situation that he was enduring could not have been changed. But he uses the word *stégomen* which implies to cover in silence, to provide a roof over without any resistance. In 1 Corinthians 13:7 Paul, speaking of God's love in the believer's heart, says, "It endures [*stégei*] quietly and provides a roof over all disturbing attitudes." It was divine love in the heart of Paul that caused him not to accept the rightful remuneration for his ministry among the Corinthians, and he did it without complaining. Paul valued the progress of the gospel more than the comforts of life.

"So That We May Not Cause Any Sudden Interruption in the Gospel of Christ"

What I have translated as "sudden interruption" is the word *egkopḗ* (1464) derived from the preposition *en* (1722) in, implying suddenness, and *kopḗ,* cutting, from the verb *kóptō* (2875), to cut. It implies an incision or violent break or hampering, an interference, something that would cause the progress (*prokopḗ* [4297]) of the gospel to be interrupted. What we have translated "We may not cause [or furnish]" is the verb *dṓmen*, the aorist active subjunctive, first person plural of *dídōmi* (1325), to give. The aorist implies a one-time action. Paul was so sensitive that he did not want to give any occasion by which the gospel would be hindered even once. As he says in 2 Corinthians 11:9, ". . . and in all things I have kept myself from being burdensome unto you, and so **I will keep myself**." What an example Paul sets for us today!

<u>LESSONS</u>:

1. Paul stresses that there were apostles who had been working and were compensated for the work that they did. He did not depreciate them for that, but he insisted that as far as he was concerned, he preferred not to use the common practice of remuneration for spiritual work.
2. Paul insists that his decision not to receive pay did not mean that he was less than worthy, but that as an apostle he was more than worthy of the common practice.
3. Paul followed this same practice among the Philippians and Thessalonians also.

4. He did not reject pay for the work he was doing because he did not need it, but because he did not want to hamper the gospel of Christ in any way. The progress of the gospel was his utmost concern.

1 Cor. 9:13 | *Temple Workers Were Paid*

Do you not realize that those who are performing sacred work eat of the food sacrificed in the temple, and those who are assisting at the altar share in what is offered there?

In verse 7, to prove the common practice of compensation for work done, the apostle Paul brings the example of the soldier receiving pay, the vineyard farmer eating of the grapes, and the shepherd partaking of the milk of sheep. This is all secular work.

"Do You Not Realize That Those Who Are Performing Sacred Work Eat of the Food Sacrificed in the Temple?"

Paul then defends his attitude and that of others of not accepting remuneration for their spiritual work among the Corinthians. He now enters upon the examination of those who are laboring in the temple, even as he referred in verse 8 to the Law of Moses. He says, "Do you not realize [*ouk,* the absolute *ou* {3756} necessitating an affirmative answer; *oídate*, the perfect active indicative, second person plural of *eídō* {1492}, to realize, to intuitively know]?" Those who are gainfully employed in the temple are called *hoi,* the nominative masculine plural of the relative pronoun *hós* (3739), the ones; *tá*, the accusative neuter plural article of *ho* (3588); *hierá*, the accusative neuter plural of the adjective *hierós* (2413), sacred, with the implied noun *érga* (2041), works. *Ergazómenoi*, working or gainfully employed, is the same verb as found in verse 6. Those who are gainfully employed in the temple and perform sacred duties eat of the temple food. The reference here is to the heave offerings in Numbers 18:8–20 of which the priests and the Levites shared. These were agricultural products, certain portions of which were taken from the heave offering and given to the priests and the Levites (Num. 18:21–24; Deut. 14:23).

"And Those Who Are Assisting at the Altar Share in What Is Offered There"

"And those who are assisting" (*prosedreúontes*, the active participle, nominative masculine plural of *prosedreúō* [4332] derived from *prós* [4314], close to, and *hédra*, a seat), that is, those attending or serving (which refers to those who work in the sanctuary) shared, and not just the priests. These were the ones who were near the altar (*thusiastḗrion* [2379]) and received a portion of the offering (*summerízontai*, the present middle/passive, third person plural of *summerízomai* [4829], to share jointly, be a partaker). In Exodus 29:27 and Leviticus 7:34 we read of the heave tithe for the priests and the Levites, even as the heave offering of agricultural products. Paul is saying not only that the priests and the Levites receive parts of what was offered in sacrifice in the temple, but their assistants also received parts of the sacrifices. He continues to defend his position that it is not wrong for the one engaged in sacred things to derive his living from it.

LESSONS:

1. Work is work, and it should make no difference whether the work is in the temple or outside the temple.

2. Because one worked in the temple, it did not mean that he did not receive compensation from the temple.
3. Even those who assisted in the ministry received their share.

1 Cor. 9:14 | *Those Who Proclaim the Gospel Should Live by It*

In the same manner, the Lord also commanded that those who proclaim the gospel should receive their living by the gospel.

Paul has reminded the Corinthians that compensating a worker is a common, expected practice. It applies to the soldier, the farmer, and the shepherd (v. 7). In accordance with the law that God gave to Moses (v. 9), material compensation applies also to spiritual work (v. 11). It applies especially to the exercise of apostolic responsibility, as Paul did in proclaiming the gospel to the Corinthians (v. 12).

Although Paul defends his right that it is proper that every worker be compensated for work done, whether it be physical or spiritual, at the same time he presents a principle which supercedes that of natural conduct and specific instruction. The underlying principle of the apostle Paul was that he would do absolutely nothing to bring any hindrance to the gospel. Because of that, he refused to accept any compensation or payment for his labor of love from the people to whom he ministered the gospel, such as the Corinthians, the Philippians, and the Thessalonians while he was in their cities. It is evident, however, that Paul encouraged and received gifts expressing love and appreciation from believers who lived beyond his area of endeavor.

When he was in prison, Paul was not rude in refusing to accept help that was offered to him by the Philippians as we are informed in Philippians 2:25: ". . . and he that ministered to my wants." While he was in Corinth, he accepted gifts from Macedonia with a willing and thankful heart (2 Cor. 11:9).

"In the Same Manner, the Lord Also Commanded"

The right to receive compensation for work performed was something that the Lord taught. The word "Lord" in this verse indicates the Lord Jesus Christ (1 Cor. 8:6). He is never presented as being in conflict, but always in full agreement with anything that the Father ordained (John 14:9, 10).

"In the same manner" is a translation of the adverb *hoútō* (3779), thus, in this way. "Also" translates the conjunction *kaí* (2532), and, which, in this instance, stands for "also." This brings to mind Matthew 5:17 where we are told that the Lord did not come to destroy the law but to fulfill it.

Here in verse 14, Paul uses the verb *diétaxe*, the aorist active indicative, third person singular of *diatássō* (1299) which is derived from the preposition *diá* (1223), implying discernment, and *tássō* (5021), to arrange. It means to command, to ordain, and is spoken of Jesus and His twelve disciples (Matt. 11:1).

In Luke 17:7–10 we find a unique parable that the Lord gave to illustrate faith and duty. This was in answer to the request of the disciples to have their faith increased. He spoke of a slave who worked all day in the field, and when he returned home, the master asked him to prepare supper for him. In verse 9, the Lord poses a question as to whether or not the master would thank the servant because he simply did those things which he was commanded. The phrase "those things which are commanded" is expressed by the participial plural noun *diatachthénta*, the aorist passive participle, accusative neuter plural of *diatássō*. His answer was that he did not think so since those things, the plowing of the field and the preparation of the supper for his master, were tasks which constituted his duty. And then, in verse 10, Christ said, "So likewise you, when you shall have done all those things which are commanded you [*tá diatachthénta*], say, 'We are unprofitable servants. We have done that which was our duty to do.' " In this parable, our Lord calls the servant who only does what he is commanded to do, and not what he perceives to be his duty out of love for his master, an unprofitable servant.

"Those Who Proclaim the Gospel Should Receive Their Living by the Gospel"

It is true that the Lord commanded that the worker is worthy of his hire (Luke 10:7). This means that each piece of work is to be compensated adequately by certain pay which the worker hopes to receive and which every human employer is expected to give. The word used is *misthós* (3408), wages. In Matthew 10:10, in the expression "worthy is the worker of his food" (instead of "wages" as in Luke), we have the word *trophḗ* (5160), nourishment, sustenance. Each worker is supposed to receive adequate sustenance. The word "worthy" in Greek is *áxios* (514) which indicates inherent value, as contrasted to *tímios* (5093), worthy from the point of view of the employer. The inherent value of something is *axía* which is not found in the New Testament; but the related verb *axióō* (515), to count worthy, and the adjective *áxios*, worthy or estimated in its inherent value, and the adverb *axíōs* (516), worthily or according to its inherent value, are found. However, the word *timḗ* (5092) is attributed value or subjective value. Suppose a watch is worth only $50, but it has sentimental value for the possessor, and he may value it at $10,000. Thus work may have a generally estimated inherent value. When, therefore, the Lord says, "worthy" (*áxios*) is the worker of his own wages or food, it refers to the minimum wage that every worker should expect for a certain amount of work done.

Minimum wage, however, does not bring an abundance of satisfaction. A worker wants his work to be appreciated by the one who commissions him. The challenge of a worker is to please the master: the more the master is pleased, the more he will esteem his worker, and the more the master will recompense him. This was the philosophy of work which the apostle Paul had. He did not want to be an unprofitable servant, but a fruitful one. His philosophy is summarized in Romans 15:16, "That I should be the minister [*leitourgón* {3011}, a public servant] of Jesus Christ to the Gentiles, ministering [*hierourgoúnta*, the accusative present active participle, masculine singular of *hierourgéō* {2418}, to perform as if it were the work of a priest] the gospel of God, that the offering up of the Gentiles might be acceptable, being sanctified by the Holy Ghost." Paul's anxious concern was that the Gentiles who were finding Christ as a result of his labor among them would be a people characterized by holiness. Therefore, he did not in any way want to become a stumblingblock to them. He would not be satisfied to simply be a priest performing his prescribed duties and getting a salary for it. He was not a hireling, and he did not want anyone to make such an accusation against him.

Paul does not go contrary to the commandment of Christ, but beyond it, serving as a bondslave (*doúlos* [1401]), which he often calls himself (Rom. 1:1; Titus 1:1). As such, he always wanted to show his relationship with the Lord, and to demonstrate that he was not simply a hireling. Paul had in mind the dishonor that many preachers brought to the name of Christ while they ministered in Corinth. In 2 Corinthians 2:17 Paul called them "peddlers" of the Word of God. The word is *kapēleúontes*, the present active participle, nominative masculine plural of *kapēleúō* (2585), to profiteer. They were people who sought to profit from peddling the Word of God. Paul never wanted to give any reason to be accused that he was preaching the Word of God for the sake of gaining the favor of the rich Corinthians.

Jesus, indeed, taught that there are those who are called to proclaim the gospel full-time and to accept payment for their labor from those to whom they preach. They are worthy of our respect and help.

LESSONS:

1. Paul is not defying the commandment of Christ by refusing to be paid for his labor of love among the Corinthians.
2. Christ gave a direct commandment that those who proclaim the gospel ought to live by the gospel or the gospel treasury.
3. Those who are called by God to serve Him are worthy of our respect.

1 Cor. 9:15 | Paul Goes Beyond Simple Obedience to Christ's Commandment

I, however, did not use any such means. Nor did I write these things that such an obligation may be assumed toward me, for as far as I am concerned, I would rather die than have anyone deprive me of my boast.

In verse 12, Paul used the verb in the plural, "We did not use this privilege [*exousía* {1849}, authority]," in defending the right of the spiritual worker to be supported by those to whom he ministers. And in verse 12 he includes others, possibly Silvanus (Silas) and Timothy as not having used the apostolic authority.

"I, However, Did Not Use Any Such Means"

Now in verse 15, Paul uses the emphatic "I" (*egṓ* [1473]), drawing the contrast between others and himself. He speaks only of himself as not having used any of the apostolic privileges. "Not a single one" is what is meant by the Greek adjective *oudení*, the dative neuter singular of the adjective *oudeís* (3762), not a single one of these privileges. The statement here is rather absolute. It is as if Paul were saying to the Corinthians who accused him of not being an apostle (v. 1), that he, himself, did not use any, not a single one, of the apostolic privileges. This is a definite precaution that he took in not giving the Corinthians any reason to make spurious charges against him. From the Philippian

Christians he received gifts on two occasions while he was in Thessalonica (Phil. 4:15, 16), but from the Corinthians he would not accept anything since they did not recognize his apostleship. If the verb is taken to be *echrēsámēn* (5531) of the TR, then it would agree with the aorist tense used in verse 12. It would mean that at no time in the past did Paul use any apostolic authority among them, and especially the right to receive compensation from them while he was working among them. If, however, the verb is taken in the perfect *kéchrēmai* of the Nestle's Text, it would mean that he did not use such authority in the past and he continued not to use it. The question is whether Paul is now pleading for the recognition of his apostleship in an effort to change the attitude of the Corinthian Christians toward him and his own attitude toward them.

"Nor Did I Write These Things That Such *an Obligation* May be Assumed Toward Me"

We cannot believe Paul was seeking the support of the Corinthians since he wrote in the second sentence of this verse: "Nor did I write these things that such an obligation may be assumed toward me." "Such an obligation" is translated from the word *hoútō* (3779), meaning thus, in this way. The translation thus rendered would reduce an apostolic privilege to an obligation. The verb is *génētai*, the aorist deponent subjunctive, third person singular of *gínomai* (1096), to become, which means to take place at a particular time and then to continue. We prefer to translate this as "may be assumed toward me." The word *égrapsa,* the aorist of *gráphō* (1125), to write, carries the meaning, "I am now writing to you."

"For as Far as I Am Concerned"

Paul did not write to the Corinthians to shame them into doing that which an apostle deserves and thus, indirectly, recognize his apostleship. He worked among them without the benefit of proper recognition. What is admirable about Paul among the Corinthians, however, was that in spite of their not recognizing and not properly deeming him as an apostle, he nevertheless did not desert them nor consider them unworthy of such a ministry.

"I Would Rather Die Than Have Anyone Deprive Me of My Boast"

Paul persevered in his work for the Lord among the Corinthians and his desire to accomplish something for Him was reason to boast. The word "boast" (*kaúchēma* [2745]), with the exception of Hebrews 3:6, is used only by Paul (Rom. 4:2; 1 Cor. 5:6; 9:15, 16; 2 Cor. 1:14; 5:12; 9:3; Gal. 6:4; Phil. 1:26; 2:16). In 2 Corinthians 1:14 Paul says, "As also you have acknowledged us in part [not attributing to him full apostleship] that we are your rejoicing [*kaúchēma*, boast], even as you also are ours in the day of the Lord Jesus." The boast of Paul was that in spite of the fact that he was only partly acknowledged as an apostle, his work was effective among them. Consequently, in the day of the Lord Jesus when all believers shall appear before the judgment seat of Christ (2 Cor. 5:10), the Corinthians will be boasting of Paul and the work that he persisted to do among them. Paul declares to the Corinthians that he would rather be dead than quit doing the work that the Lord had called him to do among them, in spite of the lack of recognition and appreciation. In 2 Corinthians 1:12 Paul summarizes the reason for his rejoicing: "For our rejoicing [*kaúchēsis* {2746}, the act of rejoicing or boasting] is this, the testimony of our conscience, that in simplicity and godly sincerity, not with fleshly wisdom, but by the grace of God, we have had our conversation [conduct] in the world, and more abundantly toward you."

Paul would rather die than turn from the call of Christ to preach the gospel among the Corinthians. His boast was that in spite of the attitude of the Corinthians, he persisted in his work among them. The verb "boast" or "glory" is *kaucháomai* (2744), and, except for James using it twice, the apostle Paul uses it thrity-six times of which twenty-six times it is found in the Corinthians epistles. His philosophy of life was that our only reason for boasting is in the Lord (1 Cor. 1:31; 2 Cor. 10:17). To do the will of God through the enablement of Jesus Christ was for the apostle Paul reason to rejoice, in spite of the lack of recognition and practical support. Paul's principle of life was "for me to live is Christ, and to die is gain" (Phil. 1:21). His only reason to live was to make Christ known, and if he could not do that, he would rather be dead than alive.

What did Paul mean by saying that no one should deprive (*kenṓsē*, the aorist active subjunctive, third person singular of *kenóō* [2758], to empty) him? It is a word used exclusively by the apostle Paul in Romans 4:14; 1 Corinthians 1:17; 9:15; 2 Corinthians 9:3 and Philippians 2:7. For instance, in 1 Corinthians 1:17, Paul says, "For Christ sent me not to baptize, but to preach the gospel: not with wisdom of words, lest the cross of Christ should be made of none effect [*kenōthḗ*, the aorist passive subjunctive, third person singular of *kenóō*]." The apostle Paul rejoiced to live to make Christ known, whether or not he received the proper recognition and consequent compensation. The glory was that much greater, particularly for him, in view of the fact that no one among the Corinthians could point to him and say he was preaching for the sake of the compensation that he would receive from these wealthy people, since he received none.

LESSONS:

1. Paul does not hesitate to say that he did not receive any apostolic privilege from the Corinthians.
2. He made this peculiarity his boast because he wanted to contribute his services to the progress of the gospel among the Corinthians (v. 1).
3. He did not try, through his writing, to make them change their attitude and thus support him.
4. His rejoicing or boasting was that he could preach the gospel in spite of the objection to his apostolicity and of the neglect of their responsibility toward him.
5. He would not permit anyone to deprive him of the privilege of preaching the gospel without compensation in conformity to the dictates of his conscience.

1 Cor. 9:16 | *Preaching the Gospel For Paul Was a Necessity*

For if I preach the gospel, this is no ground for boasting. This I do of necessity. Woe, therefore, to me if I preach not the gospel.

Paul has been defending the right of Christian workers to be supported by those to whom they minister. Nevertheless, he does not avail himself of this privilege, as he did not want to be accused that he was ministering to the wealthy Corinthians out of a materialistic motive. It seems such criticism had been made in the past, and Paul was eager to avoid even the appearance of evil.

"For if I Preach the Gospel, This Is No Ground for Boasting"

The words "boast" (*kaúchēma* [2745]) and "boasting" or the act of boasting (*kaúchēsis* [2746]) as well as the verb "to boast" (*kaucháomai* [2744], or as the KJV has it, "to glory") are Pauline words. He uses them in a special sense to indicate that it is not merely an inherent duty for the Christian to boast of or glory in the Lord, but it is an imperative of the purified and trained Christian conscience. Thus in the above verse, Paul declares, "For if I preach the gospel, this is no ground for boasting." Every believer, let alone an apostle as was Paul who had been chosen by the Lord, considers evangelizing as his primary duty of life. It ought to be borne in mind that what we translated as "I preach the gospel" is the verb *euaggelízomai* which is the middle voice of *euaggelízō* (2097), to proclaim good tidings. The word is made up of the adverb *eu* (2095), well, and the verb *aggéllō*, to proclaim or tell forth. In our text, the verb is *euaggelízōmai* which is in the subjunctive mood. Thus, this means to evangelize in the present circumstance or at the present time and refers to Paul's Corinthian missionary expedition. He is saying that if he simply came to Corinth to preach the good tidings of the gospel, and that is all that he came to do, it is not something about which he should boast. He intimates that the reason he came was to do much more than that.

In 2 Corinthians 1:12 Paul explicitly speaks of his conduct among the Corinthians as being "in simplicity" (*haplótēti*, the dative feminine singular of *haplótēs* [572]), a word which has a double meaning in the New Testament. The first is simplicity, sincerity, as rendered in the KJV, but also it means liberality (2 Cor. 8:2; 9:11, 13; 11:3; Eph. 6:5; Rom. 12:8; Col. 3:22). We render the expression *en haplótēti* with the second meaning of "generously," for the attitude of Paul among the Corinthians was certainly generous. He would not accept anything as compensation for the spiritual work that he had done among them. His generosity was possible due to his simplicity of life. To do otherwise, in his own opinion and conscience, would have invalidated his work of evangelization among them. The second reason we prefer to translate *haplótēs* as "generosity" and not "sincerity" or "simplicity" is that the second word that Paul uses in this verse is *eilikrineía* (1505) which has the single meaning of sincerity. Paul, among the Corinthians, was both generous and sincere. Both of these qualities of conscience were of God.

The conscience is that internal value system that God has put in the innermost part of man to commend or to condemn him for certain attitudes and practices that he embraces. The word for "conscience" is *suneídēsis* (4893), co-perception, derived from *sún* (4862), conjointly together, and the verb *eídō* (1492), to perceive, to intuitively know as the result of a relationship established, to realize in one's spirit. Only in man did God put this conscience. The spirit which God has placed only in man knows whether something he does is right or wrong, and to what degree.

In two instances Paul describes the kind of conscience the Lord developed in him. In Acts 23:1 in speaking to the Sanhedrin, he said, ". . . men and brethren, I have lived in all good [*agathḗ,* the dative feminine singular of the adjective *agathós* {18}, benevolent] conscience before God until this day." So Paul's conscience was not only blameless (*kalḗ* [2570]), but also was benevolent (*agathḗ*), In Acts 24:16, Paul, speaking before Felix, said, "And herein do I exercise myself, to have always a conscience void of offense [*apróskopon* {677}, not taking or giving offense] toward God, and toward men." Paul declares that he was careful that his behavior and thoughts would not provide any cause for offense. This is certainly true of his life and behavior in the midst of the Corinthians. There was nothing that he did among the Corinthians that anyone could point to as a testimony of condemnation.

Paul further described his conduct as one "not with fleshly wisdom, but by the grace of God" (2 Cor. 1:12). In other words, if he were governed by the flesh, he would desire to be compensated by the Corinthians as much as possible and disregard any possible misunderstanding. He was able, however, to be generous and sincere among them because of the work of the grace of God in his heart.

"This I Do of Necessity"

Paul goes on to express his philosophy of life generally in the world and particularly among the Corinthians. The literal translation of the Greek text is "for [*gár* {1063}] a necessity [*anágkē* {318}, constraint] is laid upon [*epíkeitai*, the present middle/passive deponent indicative, third person singular of *epíkeimai* {1945} from the preposition *epí* {1909}, upon, and *keímai* {2749}, to lie on] me [*moi* {3427}]." The apostle Paul declares that evangelization is a necessity or requirement laid upon him. Every believer is required to share his faith with others, and it is a duty of which he cannot boast. But Paul's evangelizing in his exceptional way was something different. He was laboring among the Corinthians, receiving no pay while he was in personal need. He worked with his own hands to scrape together enough money on which to live. He showed great sincerity, living in simplicity, and simultaneously being able to be generous. To preach the gospel in this manner presented him with an opportunity to boast.

"Woe, Therefore, to Me if I Preach Not the Gospel"

Here in verse 16 Paul makes sure that he speaks for himself when he says, "Woe, therefore, **to me**, if I preach not the gospel." This is not ground for boasting for me (*moi*, the dative singular of the personal pronoun *egṓ* [1473], I), was Paul's attitude. The simple proclamation of the gospel for others may have been reason for boasting, but not for Paul. For him to proclaim the gospel was to demonstrate a life that had been changed by the gospel, a life not of the flesh but of the Spirit, a life willing to sacrifice and suffer for his Lord.

To show that he never entertained the idea of quitting his ministry of evangelization because of lack of support he adds, "Woe, therefore, to me if I preach not the gospel." He denounces this possibility with the interjection of grief and indignation, *Ouaí* (3759), woe, alas! This is the same denunciation our Lord used repeatedly when He condemned the hypocritical Pharisees (Matt. 23:13–16, 23, 25, 27, 29). For the third time in this verse, Paul uses the dative personal pronoun *moi*, implying God's anger and wrath against him if he were to think of giving up preaching the gospel due to financial difficulties encountered in Corinth.

For the second time he uses the suppositional conjunction of reality *eán*, "if." The "not" is the relative negative *mḗ* (3361). He uses this relative negative to show that it was within human possibility that he would quit but for the grace of God (2 Cor. 1:12). His determination to persevere in the task of evangelization in spite of all difficulties gives him ample ground for boasting.

LESSONS:

1. Paul considered evangelizing others as the basic duty of every believer, and it was even more the duty of an apostle such as he was.
2. Since evangelization is a common duty of all believers, it is no cause for boasting.
3. Paul, however, did more than evangelize among the Corinthians as 2 Corinthians 1:12 indicates. His evangelization was prompted not only by a sense of duty, but by his own conscience.
4. He served not the Corinthians, but the Lord Jesus Christ among the Corinthians.
5. His conduct was generous and sincere.
6. To Paul, evangelization was a necessity, not a choice.
7. Paul considered anything other than evangelization as incurring the wrath of God.

1 Cor. 9:17 — *Willing and Unwilling Service*

For if I do it willingly, I have a reward; but if unwillingly, I simply discharge a trust.

In the previous verse, Paul stresses the necessity of preaching the gospel and the grief that he would experience if he failed God in this area. In reality, witnessing is a requirement of all believers, but how many of us are faithful in this requirement?

"For If I Do It Willingly"

The apostle Paul, having used the conjunction of reality *eán*, "if," twice in verse 16, now begins this verse with the subjective conditional conjunction *ei* (1487), if, for the case of presenting his argument, not only for his voluntary service but also for the reason he performed it without remuneration. "If, therefore, I do this willingly, I have a reward." The word "willingly" is the Greek *hekṓn* (1635), voluntarily. The only other place in the New Testament where the adjective occurs is Romans 8:20 where Paul speaks of the fallen creation and the involuntary reaping of the consequence of man's sin. He writes, "For the creation [*ktísis* {2937}] was made subject to vanity, not willingly [*ouch*, the absolute *ou* {3756}, 'not,' which receives the consonant *ch* because the next word begins with an aspirated vowel; *hekoúsa*, the feminine of *hekṓn*, willingly], but by reason of Him who has subjected the same in hope." Paul speaks here of the involuntary suffering from the consequences of sin.

In 1 Corinthians 9:17, Paul speaks of God's election of him on the road to Damascus, not only to follow Jesus but also to serve Him. As Paul preached to King Agrippa, he said of this encounter on the road to Damascus that the Lord not only appeared to him, but He said, "Rise, and stand upon your feet: for I have appeared unto you for this purpose, to make you a minister [*hupērétēn*, the accusative masculine singular of *hupērétēs* {5257}, a subordinate attendant, a servant of lowest rank, an underrower] and a witness of these things which you have seen, and of those things into which I will appear to you" (Acts 26:16). For most of us, when the Lord calls us to Himself, He does not necessarily call us to full-time ministry. But the Lord called Paul not only to follow him, but to serve Him, and He told Paul that He would make him a servant, the humblest of the humble. The Lord did not offer Paul a chance to refuse. He made him a willing bondslave ready to plunge into anything He had for him. In fact, in Acts 26:16, what is translated "to make you" is the verb *procheirísasthai*, the aorist middle deponent infinitive of *procheirízomai* (4400) derived from the preposition *pró* (4253), before, and *cheír* (5495), hand, meaning to hand forth as if completely prepared for the task appointed to him. At the end of his life, as Paul was ready to be executed for his faithfulness in preaching the gospel, he wrote in 2 Timothy 4:6, 7, "I am now ready to be offered. The time of my departure is at hand. I have fought a good fight, I have finished my course, I have kept the faith." This is what God called Paul to be and do. As he looked forward to what awaited him, he wrote in the eighth verse, "Henceforth there is laid up for me a crown of righteousness, which the Lord, the righteous judge, shall give me at that day: and not to me only, but unto all them also that love his appearing." It is interesting, indeed, that Paul designates the crown that he is going to receive as "a crown of righteousness [*dikaiosúnēs,* the genitive of *dikaiosúnē* {1343}, righteousness]."

We find in the parable of the laborers that our Lord gave to us in Matthew 20:1–16 that the volunteer laborers whom He called without promising any specific reward, in contrast to the first ones who were hired for a specific sum, were only told that they were going to receive from Him that which was just (*díkaion*, the accusative neuter singular of the adjective *díkaios* [1342], just, righteous). That proved to be far greater than the specific reward which the first group of workers were promised and received. It means that obedience to the unconditional call to service is better than any specific reward or promise. The service which the apostle Paul was rendering to Christ was unique. It was a service based on the righteousness of Christ. Paul was ready to do anything for Christ unconditionally, and what he saw awaiting him at the end of his life was a crown of righteousness. Paul is saying, "If I do this willingly [in spite of the fact that I was conscripted], I have a reward."

The second word that we must analyze which we find in the first phrase of our verse is the verb "do" which in Greek is *prássō* (4238), to perform, to do. This verb is used more often of evil deeds or conduct, meaning to commit, to practice (Luke 22:23; 23:15, 41; John 3:20 [TR]; 5:29; Acts 25:11, 25; 26:31; Rom. 1:32; 2:1–3; 7:19; 13:4; 2 Cor. 12:21; Gal. 5:21). It stands in contrast to *poiéō* (4160) which mostly means to perform good acts. This may refer to the humble task Paul was called to perform as the lowest servant (*hupērétēs*, an underrower, a hidden rower on a boat which had two levels of rowers). Not only did he accept conscription to service, but the humblest service.

"I Have a Reward"

Paul states that he had been adopted into the family of God as a son (Rom. 8:15). He is not only a bondslave who volunteered and, as such, could expect to be rewarded, but as he says, "I have a reward." The word for reward is *misthós* (3408), wages, pay. The apostle Paul did not specify a salary in working among the Corinthians, nor would he accept one. But at the end of his life, he fully expected to receive the crown of righteousness or justice as did the volunteer laborers in the parable of the laborers in Matthew 20:1–16 (see chapter 7 of this book). Thus, he states in 1 Corinthians 9:17 that if he voluntarily did this service, he would have pay. That was certain. But he was not satisfied with pay commensurate to the work he did. He was not satisfied with specific work for specific pay. He was not working just for a salary! He was working for his Lord who rewards His servants liberally in the performance of their task.

"But if Unwillingly"

Paul enters into the second supposition, again with the subjective suppositional conjunction *ei*, as in the first phrase. He uses the contrasting particle *dé* (1161), but. "But if unwillingly [*ákōn* {210}, unwillingly, which is used only here], I simply discharge a trust." The apostle Paul was not asked whether he would serve the Lord, he was conscripted and had no choice. This made him a unique apostle. Nevertheless, he joyfully accepted the duty laid upon him in love for his Lord, as a loyal patriot willingly goes in defense of his country in time of need.

This is why Paul, at the beginning of several of his epistles, states that he is an apostle "through the will of God." This is translated from *diá* (1223), through, by; *thelḗmatos*, the genitive neuter singular of *thélēma* (2307), will, active volition, wish, good pleasure, executive will as contrasted with *boulḗ* (1012), resolve, decision; *Theoú*, the genitive masculine singular of *Theós* (2316), of God, implying the Triune God as distinguished from God the Father which would have been implied by the definite article *toú* as in John 1:1b (see 2 Cor. 1:1; Eph. 1:1; Col. 1:1; 2 Tim. 1:1).

Two words used in our verse in an adverbial sense and that occur only here are "willingly" (*hekṓn*), meaning gladly or volitionally and usually standing in contrast to coercion or compulsion (see Rom. 8:20), and "unwillingly" (*ákōn*), meaning against one's will, forced. They are related in meaning to the noun *thélēma*, will, executive will. Paul, as he begins his first and second epistles to the Corinthians, among others, asserts the fact that he is an apostle, although he did not choose to be one. Rather he was chosen by God the Father, the Son, and the Holy Spirit. As his call to faith was irresistible, so was his call to apostleship. He was in the truest sense conscripted by the divine will.

"I Simply Discharge a Trust"

Not only did God confront Paul to save him, but at the same time He called him and entrusted him *(pepísteumai,* the perfect passive indicative, first person singular of *pisteúō* [4100], to entrust, used transitively meaning to commit in trust to someone). Paul speaks of God as having entrusted him with something. What was it? In Galatians 2:7 Paul says, "But contrariwise, when they saw that the gospel of the uncircumcision was committed unto me [*pepísteumai,* entrusted] as the gospel of the circumcision was unto Peter. . . ." (See also Rom. 3:2.) Paul definitely says that God entrusted preaching to the Gentiles to him, even as Peter was entrusted with preaching the gospel to the Jews. Paul places himself in equal rank with Peter, but differentiates his mission as preaching to the Gentiles. This does not mean that Paul was to preach the gospel to the Gentiles exclusively. In fact, in his missionary journeys we find him first visiting the synagogues in local places. It was so in Corinth, as we find the record in Acts 18. We read in verses 6 and 7a, "And when they opposed themselves, and blasphemed, he shook his raiment and said unto them, 'Your blood be upon your own heads; I am clean: from henceforth I will go unto the Gentiles.' And he departed thence." Thus Paul fulfilled his trust under persecution.

What God entrusted to Paul he calls an endowment (*oikonomía* [3622]). The word is derived from *oíkos* (3624), house or property, and the verb *némō,* to deal out, distribute, apportion. *Oikonomía* was a property or a business over which a slave (*doúlos* [1401]) was placed in charge, and he was called an *oikonómos* (3623), steward or business manager. What God wanted done with His property, the gospel, His special endowment insofar as the Gentiles were concerned, He entrusted to Paul. God laid the endowment, as it were, in Paul's lap. This Paul realized, and he wanted others to realize it. In 1 Corinthians 4:1 he wrote, "Let a man so account of us, as of the ministers [*hupērétas*, the lowest servants, underrowers] of Christ, and stewards [*oikonómous*, in charge of God's property or endowment] of the mysteries of God." Thus Paul wants to be known as the lowest of the servants of Christ and the one in charge of a particular trust, the preaching of the gospel unto the Gentiles.

In order to make the sentence complete, we should borrow the idea from the next verse. If the Lord has put us in charge of an endowment, He expects us to be found faithful in fulfilling our duty. In other words, we may prove ourselves to be responsible with the task with which the Lord has charged us.

LESSONS:

1. Paul asserts that he is not a hired servant expected to do a specific duty for a specific reward.
2. What he was doing was faithfully fulfilling his trust to the Lord and not certain obligations to the Corinthians.
3. He was conscripted to be placed in charge of proclaiming the gospel to the Gentiles. This endowment he was not asked to accept, but he was found trustworthy to be committed with it (Luke 17:5–10).

1 Cor. 9:18 | *Paul Was Careful Not to Abuse His Apostolic Privilege*

What then is my pay? That I may preach the gospel of Christ without charge for the purpose of not misusing my authority in the gospel;

There could not be any earthly reward which would adequately compensate the devotion with which the apostle Paul executed the management of God's endowment. Nor did Paul want any remuneration. His service was an act of love to his Lord.

"What Then Is My Pay?"

The first thing the apostle asserts, then, is that no payment could be adequate reward for the faithful execution of his call to preach the gospel. "What [*tís* {5101}, the nominative masculine singular interrogative pronoun, implying a specific reward] then [*oún* {3767}, therefore, then] is [*estín*, the present indicative, third person singular of *eimí* {1510}, to be] my [*ho* {3588}, the masculine article 'the' implying 'my'] pay [*misthós* {3408}, salary, wages]?" This is the same as if Paul were positively stating that there is no earthly salary that could adequately compensate him for what he was doing for God; therefore, receiving such a salary was not his concern. His dedication to the Lord could not be bought.

"That I May Preach the Gospel of Christ Without Charge"

On the other hand, Paul's concern was "that I may preach the gospel of Christ without charge." The sentence begins with the conjunction of purpose and determination, *hína* (2443), in order that. The verb that goes with this conjunction is *thḗsō*, the aorist active subjunctive, first person singular of the verb *títhēmi* (5087), to put, place, make, which in this instance is the gospel (*tó*, the accusative neuter singular article of *ho* [3588], the; *euaggélion* [2098], gospel). Paul uses "the gospel of Christ" for the second time in this verse, as in verse 12. He also uses the expression in 2 Corinthians 2:12; 9:13; 10:14. He is particularly stressing the gospel, not of the incarnate Jesus, but of the divine Messiah who revealed Himself to Paul after His resurrection. Paul was determined to preach the gospel without charge (*adápanon* [77], costless, from the privative alpha [*a* {1}], without, and *dapánē* [1160], expense). This is the only place that the word is found in the New Testament. Paul is not teaching here that a minister of Christ is not entitled to compensation (1 Cor. 9:13, 14), but that he, himself, wanted to so serve his Lord. He wanted his evangelizing or preaching of the gospel (*euaggelizómenos*, the present middle participle, nominative masculine singular of *euaggelízō* [2097], to evangelize or preach the gospel) to be without charge. He considered the preaching of the gospel such a high calling that no one could adequately compensate him for it.

"For the Purpose of Not Misusing My Authority in the Gospel"

In the third statement that he makes in this verse, Paul gives the reason why he wants to preach the gospel without charge: "For the purpose of not misusing my authority in the gospel." The phrase "for the purpose of not" translates the Greek phrase *eis tó mḗ* (*eis*, a preposition of purpose [1519] equivalent to *hína*, so that, used in the second sentence of this verse; *tó*, the accusative neuter singular article; *mḗ* {3361}, the relative "not"). He uses the relative *mḗ* to show that as a human being, it is possible to abuse this authority, and it is only by the grace of God that he does not. The verb "misuse" is *katachrḗsasthai*, the aorist middle deponent infinitive of *katachráomai* (2710) used only here and in 1 Corinthians 7:31. It is derived from *katá* (2596), against, denoting wrong or excess, and *chráomai* (5530), to use. The aorist shows that he was concerned that he should not misuse his authority as an apostle even one single time. Such was the sensitive spirit of Paul. He uses the word *exousía* (1849), authority, privilege, right, for the sixth time in this chapter (see vv. 4, 5, 6, 12 [twice]). Paul considered his apostolic privilege as one that could possibly be misused, and he was careful not to bring shame to the cause of Christ.

LESSONS:

1. Paul considered the preaching of the gospel such a high calling that it could not be compensated adequately by material means.
2. His concern was to make the preaching of the gospel without charge, lest the people who heard the gospel thought it was something that could have been compensated.
3. He did not want to give a single offense in the exercise of his apostolic privilege.

1 Cor. 9:19 — Limit Your Freedom in Order to Win Souls to Christ

For though I am free from obligations to all people, nevertheless, I became a slave to all, in order to win as many as possible to Christ.

Throughout this chapter Paul claims to be an apostle (v. 1) and, as such, he had the right to be paid for his spiritual services. However, he declined to accept any compensation so that he would not give offense to anyone or an excuse to reject the gospel, which he was determined to preach without charge.

"For Though I Am Free"

In the first verse he asked the question, "Am I not free?" Here he answers it: "For though I am free [*eleútheros* {1658}, a free person; *gár* {1063}, for, though; *ṓn* {5607}, being, the present participle, nominative masculine singular of *eimí* {1510}, to be]." He stresses the responsibility that freedom entails and recognizes that it can present problems.

Paul is speaking about the freedom that he had in Christ (John 8:32, 36), that he was freed from sin (Rom. 6:18, 22; 8:2; Gal. 5:1), and that his freedom by Christ and in Christ made him a slave unto God (Rom. 6:6, 18, 22). The freedom which Paul refers to here in 1 Corinthians 9:19 is particularly the freedom from obligations to people. If he received recompense from the Corinthians, he felt he would be obligated to them. The Corinthians, being well-to-do, might try to obligate Paul to such an extent that his teaching among them would be compromised or tainted with favoritism. This may be the reason why Paul baptized very few among the Corinthians. Not that baptism was unessential, but the church in Corinth was splintered, some claiming they belonged to one group, and some to another, and baptism seems to have played a large part in this division. Paul did not want to perpetuate such divisiveness. Thus in 1 Corinthians 1:14–16 Paul says, "I thank God that I baptized none of you, but Crispus and Gaius; lest any should say that I have baptized in my own name. And I baptized also the household of Stephanas: besides, I know not whether I baptized any other."

"From *Obligations to* All *People*"

Paul did not feel that he was morally obligated to any of the Corinthians for personal favors done for him, and thus his statement is general and inclusive: "I am free from [*ek* {1537}, of, or from] all [*pántōn*, the genitive masculine plural of the adjective *pás* {3956} which means any one individual and all of them as a group] obligations." It is as if Paul were saying, Among you all there is not one to whom I am obligated, and toward all of you I feel that I am free from obligation. Paul is particularly referring to the fact that he did not seek nor receive any material compensation for any spiritual work he did among the Corinthians.

To the contrary, many people were obligated to him for services that he had rendered to them free of charge. "To all" is how I translated *pásin*, the dative masculine plural of the adjective *pás*, all, any, anyone and all put together. Naturally, Paul is referring here to all those to whom he had somehow ministered.

"Nevertheless, I Became a Slave to All"

Having given to the Corinthians so fully and freely, Paul could say of himself, "I myself [*emautón*, the accusative masculine singular of the reflexive pronoun *emautoú* {1683}, myself, derived from *emoú* {1700}, of me, and *autós* {846}, self] became a slave to all."

To show that it was entirely a free choice of his sanctified volition, he used the verb *edoúlōsa*, the aorist active indicative, first person singular of *doulóō* (1402), to enslave. He says that he enslaved himself voluntarily to all whom he came to know and to minister. They were obligated to him in that he served them gratis, his only motivation being to please God and not to gain their favor.

"In Order to Win as Many as Possible to Christ"

Paul then goes on to express the reason he obligated everybody to himself: "In order to win as many as possible." The clause begins with *hína* (2443), that, so that, for the purpose of. This states the verb that follows to be his definite purpose. The purpose was "to win" (*kerdḗsō,* the aorist active subjunctive, first person singular of *kerdaínō* [2770], to win), meaning to win over to Christ and thus bring to salvation (v. 22). The verb *kerdaínō* is equivalent to *sṓzō* (4982), to save (see 1 Cor. 7:16; 1 Pet. 3:1). Paul knew that he could not win them all to Christ, but he wanted to win as many as possible (*toús pleíonas*, the accusative masculine plural comparative of *pleíōn* [4119], the comparative of *polús* [4183], many) through his preaching. While he knew that he could not win everyone to Christ, he did not want to lose any because of his conduct.

LESSONS:

1. Paul recognized that he had been freed from sin and enslaved to God. He did not consider himself freed by God to sin, but freed by God to be righteous and live righteously (Rom. 6:18, 22).
2. His principle of life was that he should not obligate himself to anyone by accepting favors from them.
3. He conceived it to be a safer philosophy of life to serve others as if he were a slave of their conscience.
4. He lived in such a way among the Corinthians that all were obligated to him because of his free services in preaching the gospel.
5. He adopted this philosophy of life for the single purpose of winning as many as possible to Jesus Christ.
6. He knew that there were going to be some won to Jesus Christ and to salvation, but he knew that he could not win them all. However, he did not want to lose any as a result of his untoward conduct.
7. Freedom to accept favors enslaves one's freedom.
8. Paul recognized that accepting favors from men befuddles one's righteous judgment toward those from whom he receives them.

1 Cor. 9:20 | *Paul Lived Like a Jew to Win Them to Christ*

And to the Jews, I became as a Jew, so that I may win Jews; to those under the law, I became as under the law, that I may win those under the law.

Paul was a Jew of the tribe of Benjamin and a member of the party of the Pharisees (Rom. 11:1; Phil. 3:5; Acts 23:6). He was born a Roman citizen in Tarsus (Acts 16:37; 21:39; 22:25–30), not an insignificant city of Asia Minor, for it was the seat of one of the three great universities of the ancient world. Tarsus ranked next to Athens and Alexandria.

"And to the Jews I Became as a Jew, so That I May Win the Jews"

When addressing the Jerusalem mob, Paul did not hesitate to say that he was a Jew (Acts 22:3). He did not deny his lineage. Here, however, in 1 Corinthians 9:20, he is stating that his desire was to win as many as possible to Jesus Christ. The first group he tried to win were the Jews. In Romans 10:1 he wrote, "Brethren, my heart's desire and prayer to God for Israel is that they might be saved." To express his great desire to lead his own people to Christ, he writes in Romans 9:3, "For I could wish that myself were accursed from Christ for my brethren, my kinsmen according to the flesh." He expresses his lineal descent from the Jews.

However, when Paul refers to himself as a believer in Christ in this instance, he does not call himself a Jew. Observe what he says: "And I became to the Jews **as** a Jew." He does not say, I **am** a Jew, but, I became **as** a Jew. The verb "became" is the Greek *egenómēn*, the aorist middle deponent indicative, first person singular of the verb *gínomai* (1096), to become. And the expression "**as** a Jew" is *hōs* (5613), as; *Ioudaíos* (2453), a Jew.

He did not consider himself a Jew under obligation to keep the Law of Moses, but when he lived and worked among them, he behaved as if he were a Jew for the single purpose of winning as many as possible to Christ.

"To Those Under the Law, *I Became* as Under the Law, That I May Win Those Under the Law"

To indicate that there was a difference between himself as a Christian of Jewish origin and the Jews whom he was trying to win to Christ, Paul called them "those [*toís*, the dative masculine plural article *ho* {3588}] under the law." The inference here is that the Jew is under the law, but a Christian Jew is not.

The effort of the apostle Paul was not merely to convert the Jews to Christ, but to convert those under the law that they may no longer be enslaved by the law, but free in Christ (John 8:32, 36; Gal. 3:13).

Paul does not advocate hypocrisy, but gentleness of approach. However, there should be no compromise which would lead one to believe that the law is a means to salvation instead of grace (Rom. 6:14). The law was given as the "schoolmaster" to lead them to Christ (Gal. 3:24, 25). A perfect illustration of Paul's accommodation to the Jews without compromise is the circumcision of Timothy before he took him on a missionary trip with him (Acts 16:1–4).

In almost every city Paul visited, he entered the synagogue and preached the gospel to the Jews (Acts 9:20; 13:5, 14, 43; 14:1; 17:1, 10, 17; 18:4, 19; 19:8). His philosophy of missions was accommodation to ethnic traditions without giving the impression that one could be saved by them. He clearly taught that there is no other way of salvation except believing in the death and resurrection of Christ (1 Cor. 15:3) and living in the freedom that the indwelling Christ brings, a freedom that is not license to sin (Gal. 5:1; 1 Pet. 2:16).

LESSONS:

1. Paul does not deny that he was born a Jew under the Law of Moses.
2. He does not, however, when under grace, pretend to still be a Jew, but merely ready to identify himself as a Jew for the sake of winning as many Jews as possible to Christ.
3. He was not simultaneously under grace and under the Law of Moses.
4. He was under one Master who enslaved him, and by this enslavement Christ made him free (Rom. 6:18–23).
5. Those under the law need to be liberated by Christ and be placed in Christ.

1 Cor. 9:21 | Winning Those Who Seem to Possess No Law

To the ones not having the law, I became as not having the law (not being free from the law of God, but possessed by Christ's law) that I might win those who are without the law.

In the previous chapter, Paul explained his manner of living when he was among the Jews. When with them, Paul followed their traditions, although he was a free man in Christ. This was not hypocritical; rather it was out of consideration on his part so that he might not be offensive to them.

"To the Ones Not Having the Law"

It is evident that Paul speaks here of the Gentiles who were not under the Law of Moses. The meaning becomes apparent when we have in mind 1 Corinthians 10:32 which clearly relates to this: "Give none offense, neither to the Jews, nor to the Gentiles, nor to the church of God." There are three classes of people: first, the Jews; secondly, the Gentiles; and thirdly, those who come from any race who, because of their belief in Jesus Christ, constitute the body of Christ or the church of God. When a Jew or a Gentile becomes a believer in Jesus Christ, he moves from his previous designation into the church of God. This is why, in the previous verse, Paul did not present himself as being a Jew which he was by virtue of his birth and tradition, but "as a Jew" respecting the laws that are sacred to the Jews, but not bound by them. The basic reason for his conformity to the Jewish tradition was that he might win as many Jews as possible to Jesus Christ.

Paul speaks of the Gentiles here in a circuitous way in order to denominate their nonexisting ties to the Law of Moses under which the Jews lived. He called the Gentiles whom he was trying to win *toís anómois*, "to the ones not having the law" (*toís*, the dative masculine plural article of *ho* [3588], to the; *anómois*, the ones having no law, the dative masculine plural of the adjective *ánomos* [459] which is derived from the privative alpha [*a* {1}], without, and *nómos* [3551], law). Those not bound by the Law of Moses were the Gentiles. Although these Gentiles did not consider themselves bound by the moral law, in God's sight they were sinners. In 1 John 3:4 we find the statement which includes everyone, Jew and Gentile: "Whoever practices sin transgresses also against the law: for sin is the transgression of the law." People were sinners before God gave the law. After He gave the law, people were not only sinners, but also transgressors of the law. The Gentiles, therefore, could not claim sinlessness because they were not included under the law. In the matter of who is a sinner and who is not, there are only two sides to consider—God's and man's. In the sight of God, according to Romans 3:23, "All have sinned and come short of the glory of God." This includes the Jews who not only were sinners, but also transgressors of the law. It also includes the Gentiles, who, although they did not have a law against which to sin, still they were sinners. God did not make a specific law for the Gentiles as He did for the Jews which He gave by His servant Moses. As far as the Gentiles were concerned, they were without the law, and therefore they would not be judged for their transgression of this specific law of God, but for the fact that they were sinners. As Paul says in Romans 2:12, "For as many as sinned without law shall also perish without law; and as many as sinned in the law, shall be judged by the law." As far as God is concerned, the Gentiles are sinners because, although they did not have the law against which to sin, Paul tells us that there is a law of God written not on plaques of clay, but in their hearts:

> For when the Gentiles, which have not the law, do by nature the things contained in the law, these, having not the law, are a law unto themselves: which show the work of the law written in their hearts, their conscience also bearing witness, and their thoughts the meanwhile accusing, or else excusing one another (Rom. 2:14, 15).

Therefore, the Gentiles have the law of God written in their hearts which either accuses or excuses them. This is the value system God put in the heart of man called "conscience," the ability to know together with God whether or not they are committing sin.

"I Became as Not Having the Law"

Paul does not claim in our verse that he is acting unconsciously, but that he has become as one not having the Law of Moses to govern him. He says that as he lives and endeavors to win the Gentiles to Christ, he lives as (*hōs* [5613]) if he did not have the law. He does not mean that he becomes a hypocrite, but he places himself as if he were a Gentile. He visualizes how such a person would view the gospel in an effort to determine the appropriate way to present it to him. It is the same today as presenting the gospel to a Buddhist. One must consider himself in the position of a Buddhist to be able to present the gospel accordingly, in a manner so that it can be understood and accepted in view of the tradition in which a Buddhist is found. A person does not have to become a Buddhist in order to win a Buddhist to Christ, but it is necessary to understand the mindset of the Buddhist first and then present the gospel accordingly.

"(Not Being Free From the Law of God, but Possessed by Christ's Law)"

So that Paul may not be misunderstood, he inserts a parenthetical statement: "Not being free from the law of God [*mḗ* {3361}, the relative 'not'; *ṓn*, the present participle, nominative masculine singular of *eimí* {1510}, being; *ánomos*, lawless, a transgressor; *Theṓ*, toward or against God, the dative masculine singular of *Theós* {2316}, God]."

The word *ánomos* must be understood here as going against the law of God or a transgressor against God, not simply without a law. In the three instances that the word *ánomos* occurs in the plural (Mark 15:28; Luke 22:37; Acts 2:23) it means the transgressors, particularly those transgressors by whom Jesus was to be crucified. Paul did not want to give the impression that in order to reach sinners, he himself became lawless and a transgressor against God.

So that he would not be misunderstood as a transgressor in order to reach transgressors with the gospel, Paul immediately adds the next clause which is antithetical starting with the adversative particle *allá* (235), but. This is followed by the word *énnomos* (1772) which is the exact opposite of *ánomos*. I have elected to translate this as "possessed by Christ's law." It is made of the preposition *en* (1722), in, and *nómos*, law, and is followed by *Christṓ* which is the dative of *Christós* (5547), Christ, Messiah. The dative indicates that Paul was a keeper of the law because he was in Christ. There are some texts which have the word "Christ" in the genitive, *Christoú*. This could be interpreted as being a fulfiller of the law because he is Christ's. The meaning with the dative or the genitive is essentially the same. Christ makes the difference as to whether or not a person keeps the law of God. It makes no difference whether a person is a Jew and has the law as delivered by God to Moses, or whether through the indwelling Christ he has the law of God written in his heart. Christ is the fulfillment of the law, and he who has Christ in him fulfills the law of God (Matt. 5:17).

"That I Might Win Those Outside the Law"

He who has Christ in his heart, whether a Jew or a Gentile, will have a tender conscience in the performing of the will of God in such a way that he may win as many to Christ as possible. The same way that Paul wished that he would win as many Jews to Christ as possible, here he expresses the same wish that he may win those outside the law (*anómous*, the accusative plural of the adjective *ánomos*, a transgressor or those people outside the law), the Gentiles.

LESSONS:

1. Paul recognized that the endeavor to reach Jews and Gentiles must take into account their ethical traditions and beliefs.
2. He believed, however, that it was the same grace of God that could save both Jews and Gentiles.
3. In order to reach any group, we do not have to become one of them, but we have to understand their mindset and their customs.

1 Cor. 9:22 | *Paul's Respect for The Weak*

> *To the weak I became as if I were weak in order to win the weak. I have become all things to all men, so that by all means I may save some;*

Thus far Paul spoke of the Jews and of the Gentiles, and that in his efforts to win as many as possible to Jesus Christ, he was willing to become as a Jew to the Jews or as a Gentile to the Gentiles without sacrificing in any way the basic doctrines of the Christian faith.

"To the Weak"

Paul now mentions another group, apparently prevalent in Corinth, whom he calls "the weak" (*tois asthenésin*, the dative masculine plural of the adjective *asthenḗs* [772], weak, derived from the privative alpha [*a* {1}], without, and *sthénos*, strength, derived from *sthenóō* [4599], to strengthen). *Asthenḗs* is one without physical, moral, or spiritual strength, feeble in body or soul. It is evident that Paul does not refer here to the physically ill, but the weak in faith for whom he showed great concern. In Romans 14:1 he writes, "Him that is weak in the faith you receive, but not to doubtful disputations." Paul was concerned lest his apostolic authority (*exousía* [1849], authority, right, privilege) wrongly used might become a stumblingblock to someone (1 Cor. 8:9).

In this ninth chapter he uses the word *exousía* six times in verses 4, 5, 6, 12 (twice), and 18. He believed that the strong in faith should bear the infirmities of the weak, and not please themselves (Rom. 15:1). He speaks of the weak conscience that may be defiled by the action of the strong Christian (1 Cor. 8:7).

"I Became as if I Were Weak"

Paul uses the same verb "became" as in verse 20, which is the Greek *egenómēn*, the aorist middle deponent indicative, first person singular of *gínomai* (1096), to become. He was, indeed, strong in the faith. He was well instructed and grounded in the Lord. Writing to the Philippians (4:13), he says, "I can do all things through Christ which strengthens me." What is translated "I can do all things" is the verb *ischúō* (2480), to have inherent strength. But Paul always realized that his accomplishments came only through the enablement of Christ. "Through Christ who strengthens me" is *tṓ endunamoúnti*, the present active participle, dative masculine singular of the verb *endunamóō* (1743), to strengthen. This verb derives from *dúnamis* (1411) which means accomplishing strength. Paul had in him the inherent strength of the Lord, but he realized at the same time that it was Christ who helped him to accomplish anything.

Paul's attitude among the Corinthians was not one of arrogance, rather it was winsome. It was an enlightenment of his own advice in Romans 14:1, "Him that is weak in the faith you receive." He went a step further as is implied in our text. Not only did he receive them (*proslambánesthe*, the present middle imperative, second person plural of *proslanbánō* [4355], to take to or with oneself in one's company which is derived from the preposition *prós* [4314], to, and *lambánō* [2983], to take) to himself, but he worked to instruct them in the faith that they might reach that position of maturity desired. Paul's philosophy was to treat the weak in faith in Corinth as if they were children, babies. In 1 Corinthians 3:1 Paul wrote, "And I brethren, could not speak unto you as unto spiritual, but as unto carnal [weak in faith], even as unto babes [*nēpíois*, the dative masculine plural of the adjective *nḗpios* {3516}, baby-like] in Christ." In 1 Corinthians 13:11 in which Paul embodies his philosphy of ministry, he says, "When I was a child, I spoke as a child, I understood as a child, I thought as a child: but when I became a man, I put away childish things." That is what Paul sought to be, a child among children for the purpose of seeing their growth to mature men and women in Christ. His purpose was to let love be the ruling principle of maturity, not the mere keeping of laws and traditions. Thus he wrote in Galatians 4:3, "Even so we, when we were children, were in bondage under the elements of the world." Oh, how Paul longed for the day when those he tried to reach with the gospel would grow to maturity. Thus in Ephesians 4:14 he writes, "That we henceforth be no more children, tossed to and fro, and carried about with every wind of doctrine, by the sleight of men, and cunning craftiness whereby they lie in wait to deceive." The verb *egenómēn*, I became, implies volition and selection of time at which Paul became as (*hōs* [5613]) the sick person (*asthenḗs*), without strength in order to sympathize with the one who was weak. Paul was willing to both feel his weakness and to help the weak person understand that he could be made strong.

In order, however, to help others to be strong, Paul did not disdain their weakness, but sympathized and helped them. That takes love. This is the meaning that must be attributed to the verb "to win" (*kerdḗsō* from *kerdaínō* [2770], to gain, to win). The Lord Jesus in Matthew 18:15 used the same verb when He said, "Moreover, if your brother shall trespass against you, go and tell him his fault between you and him alone: if he shall hear you, you have gained [*ekérdēsas*, the aorist active indicative of *kerdaínō*] your brother." It is also the same verb as used by Peter in his first epistle (3:1) when he says, "Likewise, you wives, be in subjection [*hupotassómenai*, the present passive participle, nominative feminine plural of *hupotássō* {5293}, to subject or to arrange in the proper category] to your own husbands; that, if any obey not the Word, they also may without the word [of the wife] be won [*kerdēthésontai*, shall be won, the future passive indicative, third person plural of *kerdaínō*]." It is evident that the verb here means to understand their lost condition and be saved. Paul declares that in order to help those who are weak in the faith, we must empathize as if we were weak ourselves. At the same time we can understand their feelings and aspirations of hope. Empathy gives love power and makes it helpful.

Several passages of Paul's epistles to the Corinthians give ample evidence of his attitude toward the weak in the faith. The first is found in 1 Corinthians 2:1–5:

> And I, brethren, when I came to you, came not with excellency of speech or of wisdom, declaring unto you the testimony of God. For I determined not to know anything among you, save Jesus Christ and him crucified [when Christ was crucified He assumed weakness although, in reality, He was not weak]. And I was with you in weakness [*en astheneía*], and in fear, and in much trembling. And my speech and my preaching was not with impassioned words of man's wisdom, but in demonstration of the Spirit and of power. That your faith should not stand in the wisdom of men, but in the power of God.

Paul declares to the Corinthians that he was assuming weakness to help the weak, although in reality he was strong in the Lord.

In the second passage in 1 Corinthians 4:9–13, Paul describes how apostles should behave toward common believers:

> For I think that God has set forth us the apostles last, as it were appointed to death: for we are made a spectacle unto the world, and to angels, and to men. We are fools for Christ's sakes, but you are wise in

> Christ; we are weak, but you are strong; you are honorable, but we are despised. Even unto this present hour we both hunger, and thirst, and are naked, and are buffeted, and have no certain dwelling place; and labor, working with our own hands: being reviled, we bless; being persecuted, we suffer it: being defamed, we entreat: we are made as the filth of the world, and are the offscouring of all things unto this day.

"In Order to Win the Weak"

Apostles should be ready to assume the least position in life in order to win as many as possible to Christ. This attitude is assumed by the apostles and the apostle Paul in particular, because they believed in the transcience of this life and the eternity of the life to come, and that the most important thing was to win souls to Christ and to make the weak in the faith strong in the Lord. Thus he writes in 2 Corinthians 4:17, 18, "For our light affliction, which is but for a moment, works for us a far more exceeding and eternal weight of glory; while we look not at the things which are seen, but at the things which are not seen: for the things which are seen are temporal; but the things which are not seen are eternal."

And in 2 Corinthians 11 through the 10th verse of chapter 12, Paul enumerates his sufferings for the sake of the gospel. In 2 Corinthians 11:29, 30, he writes, "Who is weak [*astheneí*, the present active indicative, third person singular of *asthenéō* {770}, to be sick], and I am not weak [*asthenṓ,* the present active indicative, first person singular]? Who is offended, and I burn not? If I must needs glory, I will glory of the things which concern my infirmities."

To some, Paul's philosophies of life and ministry were despicable, but to him they were glorious because they gave the opportunity to glorify Jesus Christ and not himself. Paul, as an apostle, could have claimed power and privileges, but he did nothing of the kind. He said that as among the weak, he became weak so they might understand that they can be strong through Christ who strengthens them. To Paul, it was more glorious to go down where the weak were and pull them up to safety rather than throwing a lifeline down to them.

"I Became All Things to All Men"

With the closing sentence of this verse, Paul declares his moral character. He says, "To all I have become [*toís*, to, the dative masculine plural article of *ho* {3588}; *pási*, all, the dative masculine plural of the adjective *pás* {3956}; *gégona*, I have become, the perfect active indicative, first person singular of *gínomai*, to become] all things." This is the only instance in the New Testament that the dative masculine plural article is used with *pási*, to all. Paul here is not referring to all human beings, but those particularly that divine providence brought to him to influence and win to Christ, either initially or through a closer walk with the Lord. As far as the verb *gínomai* is concerned, it is in the perfect tense and in the first person (*gégona*), and is used for the first time here and again in 1 Corinthians 13:1, 11; 2 Corinthians 12:1, and Galatians 4:16. The perfect tense indicates that sometime during his life, Paul determined what he was going to be, and by the enablement of the Holy Spirit Paul became and continued to be that, having his character divinely molded. Paul recognized that "no man is an island unto himself," but each person has his own individual character, which he molds according to his own wishes and which has its influence on society.

In Romans 14:7 Paul stated his societal philosophy of life: "For none of us lives to himself, and no man dies to himself." Paul is concerned as to how we are influenced and how we influence those with whom we live and become acquainted in the course of our lives. But while we may influence others, we are not ultimately responsible for their eternal destiny. We must shape our lives, however, in such a way that the best impact is brought upon them because of our influences. While we can influence, we cannot change the character of other people. That is God's work. Our concern should be the influence our own life has upon those who are observing us.

We must consider each one in the group of our own little societ and all of them as a whole. That is the meaning of the adjective *pási*. It is all-inclusive and yet considerate of each individual. We cannot demonstrate the character of Christ to some selectively. As God is not a respecter of persons (Acts 10:34), so we should not be if we are to show the characteristics of the character of God.

> Wherefore, seeing we are compassed about with so great a cloud of witnesses, let us lay aside every weight, and the sin which does so easily beset us, and let us run with patience the race that is set before us, looking unto Jesus the author and finisher of our faith; who for the joy that was set before him endured the cross, despising the shame, and is set down at the right hand of the throne of God (Heb. 12:1, 2).

It is interesting, indeed, to see the other Scriptures in which *gégona*, I have become, occurs in the New Testament. We find it in Paul's hymn of love in 1 Corinthians 13:1: "Though I speak with the tongues of men and of angels, and have not love [meaning God's love], I have become [*gégona*] as sounding brass, or a tinkling cymbal." Without God's love implanted and embodied in our character, we don't produce a sound that is pleasant to others, but that of a clashing instrument. Paul could say, as he said to the Ephesians (2:8), that he was saved by grace. That was the first step. He had to receive the new birth and become a child of God (John 1:12). This meant the acceptance of God's love (John 3:16), but not only did Paul accept God's love, he allowed God's love to shape his life.

And then *gégona*, I have become, is also used in 1 Corinthians 13:11 in which Paul says, "When I was a child [*nḗpios*, baby, infant] I spoke [*eláloun*, the imperfect active indicative, first person singular of *laléō* {2980}, to speak in the sense of breaking silence, to prattle as a baby] as a child, I understood as a baby, I thought as a baby, but when I became a man, I put away [*katḗrgēka*, the perfect active of *katargéō* {2673}, to make inactive, to put away] the things pertaining to a baby." The Greek word *gégona*, I have become, cannot be properly expressed in English; therefore, we render it as an aorist and not as a perfect, expressing the time that Paul ceased to be babyish and became a mature, thinking man. In other words, there was a time that Paul acted like a baby, but he ceased acting that way and ever after could be depended upon to speak as a mature man. A baby is a human being, but it is God's will that we who are born into the kingdom of God should grow up and not behave like crying, disobedient babies (1 Cor. 1:26–31).

The next instance of *gégona*, I have become, is in 2 Corinthians 12:11 where Paul says, "I have become [*gégona*] a fool [*áphrōn* {878}, without brains] in glorying; you have compelled me: for I ought to have been commended of you: for in nothing I am behind the very chiefest apostles, though I be nothing." Paul here is saying that in his ability he demonstrated that he was equal, if not superior, to those who claimed to be superapostles, but in behavior with other people he acted as an innocent baby, without malice and without hypocrisy, which others considered as foolishness. This was the character that God had molded in him so that he could voluntarily hide his abilities and his intellect, if that would win some to Jesus Christ.

The final place where the verb *gégona* is used in the New Testament is in Galatians 4:16. Paul asked of the Galatians a question as an apologetic of his behavior: "Am I therefore become [*gégona*] your enemy, because I tell you the truth?" Paul not only was considered by some as being without brains, but also an enemy because he always spoke the truth, in spite of the fact that at times the truth was unpleasant. This is why grace and truth are listed in the order in which they are in John 1:17. Truth, although it may be unpleasant, when received in the understanding of the availability of grace, becomes something to be desired, not hated, because of the possibility of its transforming power through grace. Here Paul declares his behavior to be characterized by speaking the truth, as if the truth were condemnatory only. If truth were condemnatory only, then those who heard the truth from the apostle Paul's mouth had every reason to hate him, but the truth he expressed was mixed, or prefixed, with grace. And so, although truth was condemnatory, it aimed at the redemption of the one condemned by the truth. This was the whole purpose of Paul in both winning people to maturity in Christ or, as he says in these verses, and especially this statement, "saving them."

"So That by All Means I May Save Some"

Since the purpose of the apostle Paul's lifestyle was to save some, we must now examine what he meant by "saving." The last clause of this verse begins with the conjunction of purpose *hína* (2443), *so that,* which denotes subjective purpose, or the reason for his actions. The verb is *sṓsō,* the aorist active subjunctive, first person singular of *sṓzō* (4982), to save. When reading the verb *sṓzō*, to save, one thing comes to mind—the initial salvation from sin by believing on the Lord Jesus Christ as indicated in Acts 4:12, "Neither is there salvation in any other: for there is none other name under heaven given among men, whereby we must be saved." But as one can easily see from studying the word *sṓzō* in the Scriptures, it has nine distinct meanings (see the entry in *The Complete Word Study Dictionary: New Testament,* pp. 1353–56). Since, in this particular verse, "to save" is used synonymously with the verb "to win" or "to gain" (*kerdaínō*), it must mean to win people to accept Christ. This passage does not mean that we are co-saviors with Christ. Ultimately the Lord only is the Savior. While we preach the gospel, God alone creates faith in the heart. Scripture itself supports our vehicular role here and elsewhere; thus we read, "what knowest thou, O wife, whether thou shalt *save* thy husband" (1 Cor. 7:16), "Take heed unto . . . the doctrine; . . . for in doing this thou shalt both *save* thyself, and them that hear thee" (1 Tim. 4:16) and others *save* with fear, pulling them out of the fire" (Jude 1:23).

What is translated "by all means" is the adverb *pántōs* (3843), meaning using every legitimate means from a human standpoint. Paul does not specify which means or method, but says that the love that dwells in his heart for souls and for God would not spare anything to demonstrate that winsome love that would cause people to come to maturity in Christ. Here, again, the apostle allows the method that love will choose as most appropriate for achieving the end result which is maturity in Christ. Thus we have Paul declaring that he would become whatever was necessary for the sake of winning some to Christ. The Greek is *pási*, to all; *pántōs*, by all means that are necessary, and *pánta*, the adjective "all things." Note that the definite article is preceded by the direct object *pánta*. The Greek has it, "I have become to all people, *the* all things," meaning what is legitimate and permissible as directed and inspired by divine love within his heart.

LESSONS:

1. The differentiation should be made between the aorist verb *egenómēn,* I became, and *gégona*, I have become. *Egenómēn* is flexible as dictated by the needs of an individual and the circumstances, while *gégona* refers to the mature character of the apostle.
2. In trying to help others, we must feel their weakness in order to help them acquire the strength needed.

3. In order to help others, we must first recognize their condition and utilize every legitimate means to elevate them from their position of weakness, helping them realize that the strength of the Lord which has elevated us can elevate them, too.

1 Cor. 9:23 | As Others Believe We Become Partakers of Their Joy

And this I do for the gospel, that I may become a partaker of it.

To the Jews Paul was willing to become as a Jew, and to the Gentiles as a Gentile, and to do whatever was necessary so that he might win as many as possible. As we saw by the verb "win" or "gain" (*kerdaínō* [2770]), he meant to win to salvation indicated by the verb *sṓzō* (4982), to save, and the context that follows.

"And This I Do for the Gospel"

"And this" is *toúto* (5124), this, the accusative neuter singular of the demonstrative pronoun *hoútos* (3778), this one. By "this," Paul means all that he was willing to become and endure so that he might win many to Jesus Christ. He enumerated these things in verses 19–22.

The verb that Paul uses for "do" is *poiṓ*, the present active indicative, first person singular of *poiéō* (4160), to do. It has the meaning of accomplishing either as a completed action or an action in the process of being completed. The present indicative implies that this action which Paul was currently engaged in had already been accomplished in some cases. The only reason why he would be all things to all men was to win as many as possible to

Christ and to cause them to mature in Him. The expression "for the gospel" (*diá* [1223], for; *tó*, the accusative neuter singular article of *ho* [3588], the; *euaggélion* [2098], gospel, good news, the accusative neuter singular) indicates a more active cause and motivation than the more passive expression *héneken emoú* (*héneken* [1752], on account of [with the genitive] *emoú* [2700], of me) as in Matt. 16:25. The use of the words chosen in our verse under examination indicates that winning people to Christ, and helping them to grow in Him, takes a great deal of sacrifice and effort. But there are joys associated with such sacrifices. This is expressed with the conjunction of purpose *hína* (2443), in order that, so that, or for the purpose of. The verb *génōmai*, may become, is the aorist middle deponent subjunctive, first person singular of *gínomai* (1096), to become. When someone is won to Christ it is not only the person experiencing salvation who benefits, but also the one who has ministered to him.

"That I May Become a Partaker of It"

Those who engage in evangelism and teaching know what joy is derived from seeing a soul saved and growing in the faith. Each personal sacrifice has its corresponding joy. The word "partaker" is *sugkoinōnós* (4791), a partaker together with. This is from the preposition *sún* (4862), jointly, together with, and *koinōnós* (2844), a partaker. He who communicates the gospel, while engaging in personal sacrifice to do so, also becomes a partaker in a very special way of the joy of the experience of knowing Christ and growing in Him.

LESSONS:

1. People are saved as a result of our faithful witness for Jesus Christ.
2. They are greatly affected by our personal sacrifices and by our descending, without compromise, to where they are for the sake of uplifting them.

3. Every sacrifice of comfort has its corresponding joy manifested in the power of salvation or of growth in Christ.

1 Cor. 9:24 | *Running for the Reward*

Do you not realize that of all those running in a stadium, only one receives the prize? So run as to obtain the prize.

The superficial reading of this metaphor would wrongly lead us to believe that Paul considers the Christian life a race of competition. The strongest or fastest person wins and everyone else is a loser. Taken this way, the Christian life would be an exercise in futility. Thank God, it is far from that!

"Do You Not Realize That of All Those Running in a Stadium"

A stadium (*stádion* [4712]) was a measured track of about 185 meters where athletes ran foot races. Paul must have seen the Isthmian races in Corinth in honor of Poseidon. The lesson, however, he wanted to draw from these games was not the fact that they were competitive games, but the fact that those who ran in them had to train and constantly exercise. Those who participated ran with a definite purpose in mind, and that was to receive the prize. These two things, the discipline of exercise and the purpose of participating in the games, is something that Paul calls the Corinthians to realize. He begins this verse by saying, "Do you not realize [*ouk* {3756}, the absolute 'not'; *oídate*, the perfect active indicative, second person plural of *oída* or *eídō* {1492}, to intuitively know, to realize]?" Paul calls the Corinthians to make a deduction as to the requirements of those who run in the races and the purpose for which they run. In the same way, the Christian life is presented as a race in which it is necessary to run if one wants to receive the prize at the goal. Don't you realize, Paul says, that those running in the stadium (all of them run [*tréchousin,* the present active indicative, third person plural of *tréchō* {5143}]) who want to be rewarded are not lazy, but through exercise and discipline acquire speed?

There is one word in the Greek New Testament which combines diligence, earnest effort, and speed. It is the word *spoudḗ* (4710). In our Christian lives we are required to exercise diligence, carefulness, and speed. Paul uses this word *spoudḗ*, carefulness, in 2 Corinthians 7:11:

> For behold this selfsame thing, that you sorrowed after a godly sort, what carefulness [*spoudḗ*] it wrought in you, yea, what clearing of yourselves, yea, what indignation, yea, what fear, yea, what vehement desire, yea, what zeal, yea, what revenge! In all things you have approved yourselves to be clear in this matter.

It is not permissible for the Christian to be lazy. The word *spoudḗ* stands in opposition to laziness, as in Romans 12:11: "Not slothful in business; fervent in spirit; serving the Lord." What is translated "not slothful in business" in Greek is *tḗ spoudḗ mḗ oknēroí*, which literally means in the exercise of diligence and speed, not lazy (*oknēroí* [3636], slow, lazy, slothful). In other words, laziness should not be a characteristic of the Christian life, but diligence and speed should be its evident qualities.

The verb that is used in 1 Corinthians 9:24 is *tréchō,* to run. In the Christian life all run (*tréchousin*). The running is in a stadium which is a piece of track designed for foot racing. It is of a certain length, which, if the end is reached, constitutes an achievement. When Paul spoke to the elders of Ephesus in Miletus in Acts 20:24, he said, "But none of these things move me, neither do I count my life dear to myself, so that I might finish my course [*drómon* {1408}, the noun derived from the verb *tréchō*, to run, the aorist of which is *édramon*] with joy, and the ministry, which I have received of the Lord Jesus, to testify the gospel of the grace of God." Thus the deduction is that each Christian has a divinely prescribed course to run, and it should be done diligently and carefully.

"Only One Receives the Prize"

Paul does not set before us the spirit of competitiveness with fellow Christians as being important. This is where the physical illustration breaks down when it comes to its spiritual application. In the physical races, there is competition one with another. Nowhere in the Scriptures are we told that we are in a race to overtake others who are running with us. Even the apostle Paul in 2 Timothy 4:7, at the end of his life and ministry, wrote, "I have fought a good fight, I have finished my course [*drómos*], I have kept the faith." God had a certain course that He divinely assigned for Paul to finish. That course is specific and definitive for each one of us. God has given each one of us specific abilities that we must exercise with diligence and speed, and one of the greatest satisfactions is found when we have run well and speedily to recognize that we have executed God's plan for our lives.

In a stadium a number of athletes run together, and only the one who reaches the goal first receives the prize. The word for "receives" is *lambánei*, the present active indicative, third person singular of *lambánō* (2983), to receive. When it comes to the spiritual race, however, the race is run individually, and only God knows whether each believer has utilized all the abilities that He has given him with which to run his race. And as far as the spiritual prize that the Lord has for us, the greatness and the preciousness of it is determined by the fullness of the utilization of our divine endowments. Thus Paul says of our earthly race that "Only one receives the prize." But of the spiritual race, we are aware that there are others who are running with us, and everyone has the possibility of receiving the prize. There will be an individual evaluation of our diligence and speed in running our race, not in comparison to other athletes, but as evaluated by God himself. In 2 Corinthians 5:10 Paul wrote, "For we must all [*pántas*, the plural of *pás* {3956}, meaning every believer, and not only the one who came first among many] appear before the judgment seat of Christ; that each one [*hékastos* {1538}, each one individually] may receive the things done in his body [while alive], according to that he has done, whether it be good or bad."

So when we understand the teaching of the New Testament, we find that each and every believer will be judged as to his qualifications to receive a reward at the end of the race, but these rewards will vary. In the case of earthly races, only one receives the reward (*tó*, the neuter of *ho* [3588], the; *brabeíon* [1017], prize, award) compared with all the others who ran faster than the others in the race. In Scripture, however, we do not have merely **one** reward, **one** prize, spoken of as a crown (*stéphanos* [4735], crown), for this crown is not just one crown, but an individual crown for each believer. This is further demonstrated by Revelation 3:11, "Behold I come quickly: hold that fast which you have, that no man take **your** crown." Each one has a crown prepared for him in recognition of the diligence and speed with which he ran his race. When the crowns are distributed to the believers, however, we shall have the opportunity of seeing the crowns that others have earned, and what sorrow we shall feel in our hearts as we become aware of the fact that we could have had a bigger and brighter crown had we run more diligently and more speedily. When the day comes when we are to lay our crowns before the throne or at the feet of the Lord Jesus, what a grief it will be if our crowns are small and shameful!

"So Run as if to Obtain the Prize"

The practical lesson of the illustration of the Isthmian games that the apostle brings is recorded in the last sentence of our verse: ". . . so run [*oútō* {3779}, in this way, in this manner, likewise; *tréchete*, the present active imperative, second person plural of *tréchō,* to run] as if to obtain the prize." How does every serious athlete run a race? First of all, he does not enter the race without the proper preparation. To enter the Isthmian races one had to prepare for ten full months before the occurrence. And then there was the actual running, of which the motivating force was the winning and the reward.

In the sentence, "Only one receives the prize," there is one prize and one only that, if the runner does not win, some competitor will. There is excitement about it, but a physical race is of much less consequence than the spiritual race. The human recognition of having excelled and being rewarded by men is nothing compared to the commendation "Well done!" by the Lord (Matt. 25:21, 23; Luke 19:17). This is the "well done," not of being better than others, but the "well done" of the Lord as He compares our potential, known to Him alone, with our accomplishments.

There are moments of discouragement when we see how little others do and how much they expect in human reward. And we cry out like Paul, "Or only I and Barnabas!" (see 1 Cor. 9:6). The attitude of self-sacrifice was adequately expressed by Paul in 2 Timothy 4:6–8 as he said, "For I am now ready to be offered, and the time of my departure is at hand. I have fought a good fight, I have finished my course, I have kept the faith. Henceforth there is laid up for me a crown of righteousness, which the Lord, the righteous judge, shall give me at that day: and not to me only, but unto all them also that love his appearing."

The verb "receive," however, used in the sentence "So run so that you may receive," or obtain or secure, is *katalábēte*, the aorist active subjunctive, second person plural of *katalambánō* (2638) which comes from *katá* (2596), an intensive, and *lambánō*, to take. I have elected to translate it as "secure." It refers to the reward that one seizes after concentrated and strenuous exertion of effort. The active aorist subjunctive means that the prize is to be secured only once, and that is at the end of life's race. Every step that one takes in his Christian life ought to be viewed as to how it will affect his ultimate reward when life ends. The same verb *katalambánō* occurs three times in Philippians 3:12, 13. Paul did not declare that he secured this prize during the course of his life. Philippians 3:12 says, "Not as though I had already attained [*élabon*, the aorist active indicative, first person singular of *lambánō*], either were already perfect [*teteleíōmai*, the perfect passive indicative, first person singular of *teleióō* {5048}, to complete, to bring to an end or to a goal]." Since Paul had not yet died, he had not completed his race. Then he declares what he was in the process of doing while alive, "But I follow after [*diṓkō* {1377}, to pursue, to get myself to], if that I may apprehend [*katalábō*, the aorist active subjunctive, first person singular of *katalambánō* indicating a once-and-for-all grasping or apprehension or securing]." The apprehension of the prize at the end of the road of life is to be secured only once, and it requires effort, sacrifice, and discipline, as does the winning of any competitive race. But observe what happens when the end and the prize are secured: "On this account [*eph'hṓ*, upon which] I also [*kaí* {2532}, and, also] was seized [*katelḗphthēn*, apprehended, the aorist passive indicative, first person singular of *katalambánō*] by

Christ Jesus." This means that when I reach the end of my race, the goal of my life, and I am ready to secure the prize, Christ Jesus stands at the end to receive me and secure the prize belonging to me. I apprehend and I am apprehended. And then in verse 13 Paul continues, "Brethren, I count not myself to have apprehended [*kateilēphénai*, the perfect active infinitive of *katalambánō*]." It is as if Paul were saying, I do not do the securing, Christ does it for me. He goes on: "Forgetting those things which are behind, and reaching forth unto those things which are before, I press toward the mark [*skopón*, the accusative of *skopós* {4649}, goal; *diṓkō* I pursue, meaning I aim as with a scope, with precision]." And what is the thing that he pursues with precision? "The prize of the high calling of God in Christ Jesus." The word here is *brabeíon*, prize, as in 1 Corinthians 9:24. Paul is saying that as he runs the race of the Christian life, he uses a precision instrument with which to measure everything as to what result it will have in securing the prize that the Lord is going to give to him. That was Paul's concern, and he wanted the Corinthians and the Philippians to understand that this was the reason he chose the lifestyle he did and did not take advantage of his rights as an apostle. Rather, he was laboring as a servant with utmost sacrifice that would be recompensed by the prize that the Lord was going to secure for him.

LESSONS:

1. The Christian life is like a footrace which is run in a stadium.
2. This does not mean that we are competing against other Christians, but we must examine ourselves as to how acceptably we run the race, according to the abilities and possibilities that the Lord has given us.
3. The verb "running" is used to indicate that the Christian life can never be a life of laziness.
4. In the games, only the one who won the race received the prize. In the Christian race, however, everyone receives a prize which represents

the way that he has run and what he has achieved and whether or not he has been faithful to the rules of the race.

5. Our every step in running the race ought to be taken with exactness of aim. The reward is commensurate to the effort put forth.

1 Cor. 9:25 | When Self-control Is Exercised, Victory Is Promised

But everyone who engages in athletics exercises self-control in all things. However, they do it to receive a perishable wreath, but we an imperishable one.

Agṓnes is the Greek word for athletic events such as running, boxing, wrestling, and so forth. Such took place in a stadium. They involved one contender against equal contestants with the performance of each one being measured against the performance of the others.

"But Everyone Who Engages in Athletics"

The Christian life is compared to the athletic games. This physical illustration, however, eventually breaks down in being applied to the spiritual life. Athletics are competitive games, while the Christian life is not a competition one against another. It is a struggle (*agṓn* [73]), and it is called that because it takes effort and discipline to accomplish what God has for each one to accomplish. Indeed, the struggle can be agonizing.

Agṓn and the verb *agōnízomai* (75) are words which the apostle Paul uses to describe the struggle that one has in his Christian life against the enemies of his salvation (1 Tim. 6:12; 2 Tim. 4:7, cf. Phil. 3:12–21; Heb. 12:1). I elected to translate our verse as "everyone who engages in athletics exercises [*pás*

{3956}, all; *dé* {1161}, but; *ho agōnizómenos*, the present middle/passive deponent participle, nominative masculine singular of *agōnízomai*, one exercising in athletics]." This agrees with the previous verse in which Paul uses the illustration of a race in a stadium. The first thing he calls to our attention in that verse was that he who runs has a purpose, and that is to win the prize or the contest. We saw, however, that the prize is not determined by the fact that he did better than the others and placed first, but that every Christian has a prize to receive at the end of life when he appears before the judgment seat of Christ (2 Cor. 5:10). He will be judged according to the measure to which he has utilized his God-given abilities.

"Exercises Self-Control in All Things"

As Paul enters this verse, he tells us that to qualify for a race one should be self-disciplined. This he expresses by the verb *egkrateúetai*, the present middle/passive deponent indicative, third person singular of *egkrateúomai* (1467), to have self-control, derived from *en* (1722), in, and *krátos* (2904), dominion, strength. It refers to the one who maintains his strength and does not indulge in excesses. The verb is used in 1 Corinthians 7:9 and in our verse. Both verbs, *agōnizómenos* (exercises in athletics) and *egkrateúetai* (self-control), are in the present tense which means that while someone is engaged in athletics, he is under self-control. His desire to engage in athletics is reason enough for him to exercise self-control. This self-control is exercised in all things (*pánta*, the accusative neuter plural of the adjective *pás*). Self-control (*egkráteia* [1466]) is one of the fruits of the spirit (Gal. 5:23). It is also listed in Titus 1:8 as one of the qualifications of a church elder.

"However, They Do It to Receive a Perishable Wreath, but We an Imperishable One"

But why do athletes engage in athletic games? "They do it to receive a perishable wreath." The word for "perishable" is *phthartón* (5349), corruptible. It indicates the temporal character of an earthly crown compared to the crown that a believer is going to receive at the end of his life. This will be incorruptible or *áphtharton* (862) since it is not physical nor subject to deterioration.

The reward or prize is called in verse 24 *brabeíon* (1017), a wreath or garland bestowed on victors in the contests of the Greek games as a reward. Here in verse 25 it is called *stéphanos* which means a crown of victory given in the games. The crowns were usually woven of oak, ivy, myrtle, olive leaves or flowers. It was actually a wreath which was placed upon the winner's head, and this is why we prefer to translate it as such. In contrast to the physical wreath which is corruptible, we as believers shall receive an incorruptible crown as a reward of our having run the race acceptably before God. The rewards for the athletes are earthly and temporary, whereas the rewards for the believers are eternal, of everlasting value (2 Cor. 4:16–18).

<u>LESSONS</u>:

1. The Christian life is a life of discipline and self-control.
2. In this chapter Paul argues that he was indeed disciplined in the exercise of his apostolic power and in refraining from taking advantage of anyone.
3. A Christian ought to remember that spiritual athletics require a far greater discipline for a far greater reward than physical athletics.

1 Cor. 9:26 | The Christian Life Is Not an Aimless Struggle

Yes, indeed, now as far as I am concerned, I run not as if I have no evident aim. I do not box as if beating the air aimlessly;

All of life is a struggle, a fight to reach a goal. For the believer, however, the goal is glorious and well worth the effort.

"Yes, Indeed, as Far as I Am Concerned"

In Greek, this verse begins with the personal pronoun "I" (*egṓ* [1473]). Paul now comes to personal application. The next word is *toínun* (5106) derived from *toi* (5104), truly, indeed, strengthened by *nún* (3568), now. I have elected to translate these two words "Yes, indeed, now as far as I am concerned." Paul spoke of those who were participating in the athletic games in Corinth and compared himself to them. They did it for the prize. He used the athletic games as an illustration of the race that each one of us as Christians runs.

"I Run Not as if I Have No Evident Aim"

While we do not run against others, we run so that we may fully exercise our potential, realizing that our talents are God-given. In verse 25 Paul stressed the self-control which should characterize our lives if we want to be winners. When it comes to the end of the road, athletes hope to win a wreath that is made of perishable things which fade away. We, on the other hand, receive a reward that is incorruptible. As far as Paul himself is concerned, he says, "I run [*tréchō* {5143}] not [*ouk* {3756}, the absolute 'not'] as if [*hōs* {5613}, as, with 'if' understood]." Then follows the adverb *adḗlōs* (84), "without evident knowledge of where I am going." This we have elected to translate "not as if I have no evident aim" as best rendering the meaning of the expression: that is, I don't just run for the sake of running, but I know where I am going and why I am going there. Paul wants to stress that how he lived and died would show the value of his life. No one should spend his life without a clear view that it has an end, and it will be the terminal point of opportunity.

"I Do Not Box as if Beating the Air *Aimlessly*"

Then Paul uses the illustration of boxing and says, "I box [*pukteúō* {4438}, to box, used only here] not [*ouk*, the absolute 'not'] as if beating [*dérōn*, beating, striking, the present participle of *dérō* {1194}, to strike], the air," and I have added "aimlessly" to translate the privative alpha (*a* [1]), in *adḗlōs,* meaning without manifest purpose as if it were beating an imaginary object. "Aimlessly" would translate the word *adḗlōs.*

In other words, Paul says, I run purposefully toward the goal of life, knowing where I am going and not as a boxer who is simply beating the air for the sake of exercise.

LESSONS:

1. Paul states the course of his life as running.
2. He runs for a prize at the end of his life (2 Tim. 4:6–8).
3. His daily practice is not beating the air, but accomplishing something worthwhile while he is marching toward the goal.

1 Cor. 9:27 | *Lack of Discipline Disqualifies One from Securing the Prize*

But I subject my body to visible hardship and I make it my slave, lest by any means having preached to others, I myself may become disqualified for the prize.

When one boxes, he aims at the head of his opponent and tries to give him a knockout blow, and thus win the prize.

"But I Subject My Body"

In this verse Paul continues to use the first person singular, having himself in mind. He said in the previous verse, "I do not beat the air," but I target my opponent. He starts this verse with the adversative particle "but" (*allá* [235]): "but I beat my own body." My real opponent in the race of the Christian life, Paul intimates, is my own body. The apostle emphasizes that as the body needs discipline and training in athletics, so it does in the development and achievement of the spiritual life.

The apostle viewed his own body as needing discipline and exercise. He said, "I subject my body to visible hardship." What he meant by his "body" was the material element of life consisting of body and soul. The term *sṓma* (4983), body, in this instance must be viewed as synonymous to *sárx* (4561), living flesh. The body, or the flesh of man, is part of his human nature as contrasted to his spiritual nature. When a person becomes a

Christian, he is born again of the Spirit of God, but he does not cease to have a body that needs discipline and guidance. The flesh of the Christian stands in the way of his spiritual goal. It is to the Christian believers that Paul is writing in Galatians 5:16: "This I say then, walk in the Spirit, and you shall not fulfill the lust of the flesh." When a person is saved he does not become a supernatural human being. Sin continues to dwell in him (Rom. 7:20). The possibility of sin is not uprooted, but overcome, and this overcoming is achieved by discipline and self-control, as in the case of an athlete. Bodily strength is achieved only through exercise and discipline. In writing to the Corinthians, Paul draws the contrast between the natural man (*psuchikós* [5591], psychic man) and the spiritual man (*pneumatikós* [4152], governed by God's spirit). The "natural man" is correctly translated because it represents the body of the Christian believer as he inherited it from Adam. The spiritual man is the saved man when he will be raised from the dead. Even at his death, the Christian's body is called a "natural" (*psuchikón*) body, and it is raised a spiritual (*pneumatikón*) body (1 Cor. 15:44).

Therefore, during our whole Christian life we do not become immune to sin, but victorious over sin. This victory over sin is achieved through self-control and constant exercise, which is the prevalence of the indwelling Spirit of God over the sinful nature inherited from Adam. The self-control of our body is achieved through the death and resurrection of Jesus Christ. This is why Paul, in writing in 2 Corinthians 4:10, says, "Always bearing about in the body the dying of the Lord Jesus, that the life also of Jesus might be made manifest in our body." This is the resurrection victory of the believer who always strives against the luring power of the flesh (James 1:14; 1 Pet. 2:11; 1 John 2:16).

"To Visible Hardship"

What, then, does Paul do to bring his own body under subjection? He uses two words. The first is a verb that is used only twice in the New Testament. It is the verb *hupōpiázō* (5299) which derives from *hupó* (5259), under, and *ṓps* (which is not found in the New Testament), meaning eye or face. From this word comes *ophthalmós* (3788), eye. The verb means to strike under the eye, to give a black eye, to make the physical injury felt and visible. It means exactly as we have tried to render it in the translation, to subject the body to visible hardship. The only other place that this verb is used is in Luke 18:5 with a metaphorical meaning that the widow to whom injustice was done should give a black eye to the unjust judge (not literally, of course, but through shaming him for his indifference to her problems).

"And I Make It My Slave"

The second verb is *doulagōgṓ*, the present indicative, first person singular contraction of the verb *doulagōgéō* (1396). This is derived from *doúlos* (1401), slave, servant, and *ágō* (71), to lead, bring. The compound verb means to bring into servitude or subjection or to lead as a slave. This is the only place that this verb occurs in the New Testament. Paul says that I, as a redeemed person, not only give evidence of my struggle with my body, but I lead it as a slave. I do not let it master me.

In our redeemed state we are disturbed by the flesh and its desires, but we bring them under control. Paul, in Ephesians 2:3, reminds the Ephesians of their previous unredeemed state by saying, "Among whom also we all had our conversation [conduct] in times past in the lusts of our flesh, fulfilling the desires of the flesh and of the mind, and were by nature the children of wrath, even as others." In the eighth chapter of Romans (vv. 8–13), however, he describes the victorious life by saying:

> So then they that are in the flesh cannot please God. But you are not in the flesh, but in the Spirit, if so be that the Spirit of God dwell in you. Now if any man have not the Spirit of Christ, he is none of his. And if Christ be in you, the body is dead because of sin; but the Spirit is life because of righteousness. But if the Spirit of him that raised up Jesus from the dead dwell in you, he that raised up Christ from the dead shall also quicken your mortal bodies by his Spirit that dwells in you. Therefore, brethren, we are debtors, not to the flesh, to live after the flesh. For if you live after the flesh, you shall die: but if you through the Spirit do mortify the deeds of the body, you shall live.

And in verse 14 Paul says, "For as many as are led by the Spirit of God, they are the sons of God." The word here for "sons" is *huioí*, the plural of *huiós* (5207), grown-up sons who have learned to discipline themselves as demonstrated by the fact that they hold their bodies in subjection. The discipline of the Christian life is called adoption (*huiothesía* [5206]), the acceptance as a grown-up, disciplined child. As it took ten whole months of vigorous exercise to train the body for participation in the Isthmian games, so it takes time for discipline and self-control to bring one from being a child or newly born (*téknon* [5042]) to a mature son or daughter (*huiós*). When we learn in our Christian life to be led by the Spirit which indwells us, it becomes evident in our daily conduct.

"Lest by Any Means"

What happens to the athlete who refuses to exercise self-control and discipline? Simply, when the time comes, he is not able to participate in the games. This is what happens in the spiritual realm. If one is controlled by his body and the desires of his flesh and does not subject himself to the necessary exercises, he will not receive a prize at the end of the race.

"Lest by any means" comes from the Greek *mḗ* (3361), the relative "not," and *pṓs* (4458), by any means. When taken together, *mḗpōs* (3381) has the meaning of "lest sometimes" or "lest by any means." The relative "not" is used because this conduct is quite possible in our spiritual running. Somehow, we do not heed the dangers that exist.

"Having Preached to Others, I Myself May Become Disqualified for the Prize"

The verb "preach" (*kērúxas*, the aorist active participle, nominative masculine singular of *kērússō* [2784], to preach) does not always mean to preach the gospel or evangelize (*euaggelízomai* [2097]).

To show that this preaching is to fellow believers about the disciplined Christian life, the apostle uses the word *állois,* the dative masculine plural of the adjective *állos* (243), another, which means others of the same kind as contrasted to *hetérois* (2087) which means others of a different kind. There are so many Christians today who believe they are going to qualify to receive a reward at the end of the road who will be utterly disappointed because they do not qualify. Paul is declaring that he does not want to be a preacher of a disciplined Christian life without being disciplined himself.

In the translation, I have rendered *autós*, the nominative masculine singular personal reflexive pronoun, as "I myself." This is a supposition the apostle Paul makes, implied in the aorist participle *kērúxas,* having preached. The verb is *génōmai*, the aorist middle deponent subjunctive, first person singular of *gínomai* (1096), to become. The word *adókimos* (96), disqualified, comes from the privative alpha (*a* [1]), without, and *dókimos* (1384), acceptable. This refers to the receiving of the prize at the end of the race. It has nothing to do with salvation. The opposite of *adókimos*, disqualified or unapproved, is *dókimos*, acceptable, approved. In Greece, the Naval Academy where officers are trained for the Greek Navy is called *dókimoi*, and the school is called "The School of the Approved Ones." The apostle Paul takes us to the illustration of the Isthmian games where several people were approved for running the race, but only the most qualified one received the prize. This prize is called in 1 Corinthians 9:25 a "crown." In James 1:12 we read, "Blessed is the man that endures temptation: for when he is tried [*dókimos*, approved], he shall receive the crown of life, which the Lord has promised to them that love him." These are Christians whose service unto Jesus Christ is measured by the endurance they develop against temptation and the trials of life. They will receive a crown commensurate to their disciplined Christian life. This is the reason why we translated *adókimos* as "disqualified for the prize."

The goal, the prize, the crown is before us. Let us press eagerly and strenuously onward that we may be found worthy of that "Well done, good and faithful servant. . . . Enter into the joy of your Lord" (Matt. 25:23). The eternal reward is well worth the temporary effort.

LESSONS:

1. The apostle Paul does not hesitate to speak of the disciplined life that he lived.
2. He did not hesitate to make it evident by the many things he lacked (1 Cor. 4:8–13).
3. Paul did not believe in the eradication of sin from his body, but believed in the victory that his body could have over sin.
4. He did not allow his body to control him, but he believed that the body, subject to sin, needed the control of the Spirit of God to guide it.
5. It is evident that he is writing here to believers and that he was teaching them concerning the disciplined Christian life.

6. His disciplined life found acceptance with the Lord. It is so easy, however, to fail to qualify for the prize at the end of the road due to lack of self-discipline.
7. Any sacrifice or deprivation will be well worth the reward we shall someday receive from our Lord.

Bibliography

Aitken, W. Hay. *Newness of Life.* London: John F. Shaw and Co., n.d.

Champneys, W. Weldon. *Things New and Old.* London: F. Bowyer Kitto, 1869.

Hastings, James. *The Great Texts of the Bible.* London: Waverly Book Co., Ltd., 1912.

Hodge, Charles. *Princeton Sermons.* London: Banner of Truth Trust, 1958.

Jones, J. D. *The Gospel of Sovereignty and Other Sermons.* London: Hodder and Stougton, 1914.

Liddon, H. P. *Advent in St. Paul's.* London: Longman's, Green and Co., 1896.

Lightfoot, Joseph Barber. *Horae Hebraicae et Talmudicae, Hebrew and Talmudical Exercitations,* Vol. 4. Oxford: The University Press, 1859.

————. *Sermons Preached in St. Paul's Cathedral.* London: Macmillan and Co., 1891.

————. *Sermons Preached on Special Occasions.* London: Macmillan and Co., 1914.

Lloyd-Jones, D. Martin. *The Miracle of Grace and Other Messages.* Grand Rapids, MI: Baker Book House, 1986.

Maclaren, Alexander. *Christ's Musts.* London: Hodder and Stoughton, 1905.

————. *Expositions of Holy Scripture, St. Paul's Epistles to the Corinthians.* New York: A. C. Armstrong and Son, 1910.

Moffat, Hugh B. "The Heavenward Course." In *The Pulpit, Sermons by Eminent Living Ministers,* Vol. 68. London: J.M. Robinson, 1856.

Nicoll, W. Robertson, Ed. *The Sermon Outline Bible.* Grand Rapids, MI: Baker Book House, 1958.

Parker, Joseph. *Preaching Through the Bible,* Vol. 26. Grand Rapids, MI: Baker Book House, 1959.

Redpath, Alan. *The Royal Route to Heaven.* Grand Rapids, MI: Fleming H. Revell and Co., 1960.

Robinson, Chas. S. *Studies of Neglected Texts.* New York: American Tract Society, 1883.

Simeon, Charles. *Expository Outlines on the Whole Bible.* Grand Rapids, MI: Zondervan Publishing House, 1955.

Spurgeon, C. H. *The Treasury of the New Testament*, Vol. 3. Grand Rapids, MI: Zondervan Publishing House, 1950.

———. *Storm Signals*. London: Passmore and Alabaster, 1885.

Talmage, T. DeWitt. *Every-Day Religion*. New York: Harper and Brothers, 1875.

Taylor, Albert. "Paul's Self-Training" *The Christian World Pulpit*, Vol. 80. London: James Clarke and Co., 1911.

The Publications of the American Tract Society, Vol. 5. New York: American Tract Society, n.d.

Walpole, Cecil F. "Paul's Self-Training" *The Christian World Pulpit*, Vol. 80. London: James Clarke and Co., 1911.

Wuest, Kenneth S. *Golden Nuggets from the Greek New Testament*. Grand Rapids, MI: Wm. B. Eerdman's Publishing Co., 1953.

Lexicons, Encyclopedias, and References for Greek Readers, from Classical and Koine Greek to Modern Greek

Byzantiou, S. D. *Lexikon tēs Hellēnikēs Glōssēs* (*Lexicon of the Hellenic Language*). Athens: Koromēla, A., 1852.

Dēmētrakou, D. *Lexikon tēs Hellēnikēs Glōssēs* (*Lexicon of the Hellenic Language*). Athens: Dēmētrakou, 1954.

Enkuklopaidikon Glōssologikon Lexikon (*Encyclopedic Glossological Lexicon*). Athens: Morfōtikē Hetaireia.

Enkuklopaidikon Lexikon Eleutheroudaki (*Eleutheroudaki, Encyclopedic Lexicon*). Athens: Eleutheroudakis, 1927.

Kalaraki, Michael and Nikolas Galanos. *Iōannou tou Chrusostomou Ta Hapanta* (*Complete Works of John Chrysostom*), 1899.

Liddell, Henry George, and Robert Scott. *Greek–English Lexicon*, as Translated and Enriched by Xenophōn P. Moschos and Michael Kōnstantinides. Athens: John Sideris.

Megalē Helēnikē Enkuklopaideia (*Great Hellenic Encyclopedia*). Pursos (Pyrsos), Athens: Hēlios.

Neōteron Enkuklopaidikon Lexikon Hēliou (*New Encyclopedic Lexicon "Hēlios"*). Athens: Hēlios.

Papaoikonomou, George L. *Lexikon Anōmalōn Rhēmatōn* (*Lexicon of Irregular Verbs*). Athens: Kagiaphas.

Stamatakou, J. D., *Lexikon Archaias Hellēnikēs Glōssēs* (*Lexicon of the Ancient Hellenic Language*). Athens: Petrou Dēmētrakou, 1949.

Works by Spiros Zodhiates

Editor, *The Complete Word Study Dictionary: New Testament.* Chattanooga: AMG Publishers, 1992.

The Epistles of John. Chattanooga: AMG Publishers, 1994.

List of Abbreviations

acc. (accusative)
act. (active)
aor. (aorist [2 aor. for second aorist])
cf. (compare)
ch. (chapter)
comp. (composition)
dat. (dative)
etc. (and so forth)
ff. (following)
gen. (genitive)
i.e. (that is)
imperf. (imperfect)
indic. (indicative)
inf. (infinitive)
KJV (King James Version)
MT (Majority Text)
mid. (middle)
n. d. (no date available)
N. p. (no publisher available)
NASB (New American Standard Bible)
NIV (New International Version)
NKJV (New King James Version)
nom. (nominative)
p. (page), pp. (pages)
part. (participle, participial)
pass. (passive)
perf. (perfect)
pl. (plural)
pres. (present)
pron. (pronoun)
Sept. (Septuagint)
sing. (singular)
TR (Textus Receptus)
UBS (United Bible Society)
usu. (usually)
v. (verse), vv. (verses)
vol. (volume)

GUIDE TO THE TRANSLITERATION AND MODERN PRONUNCIATION OF THE GREEK ALPHABET

Capital Letter	Small Letter	Greek Name	Trans-literation	Phonetic Sound	Example
Α	α	alpha	*a*	a	as in father
Β	β	bēta	*b*	v	as in victory
Γ	γ	gamma	*g*	y	as in yell (soft gutteral)
Δ	δ	delta	*d*	th	as in there
Ε	ε	epsilon	*e*	e	as in met
Ζ	ζ	zēta	*z*	z	as in zebra
Η	η	ēta	*ē*	ee	as in see
Θ	θ	thēta	*th*	th	as in thin
Ι	ι	iōta	*i*	i	as in machine
Κ	κ	kappa	*k*	k	as in kill (soft accent)
Λ	λ	lambda	*l*	l	as in land
Μ	μ	mē	*m*	m	as in mother
Ν	ν	nē	*n*	n	as in now
Ξ	ξ	xi	*x*	x	as in wax
Ο	ο	omicron	*o*	o	as in obey
Π	π	pi	*p*	p	as in pet (soft accent)
Ρ	ϱ	ro	*r*	r	as in courage
Σ	σ,ς*	sigma	*s*	s	as in sit
Τ	τ	tau	*t*	t	as in tell (soft accent)
Υ	υ	ēpsilon	*u*	ee	as in sec
Φ	φ	phi	*ph*	ph	as in graphic
Χ	χ	chi	*ch*	h	as in heel

Ψ	ψ	psi	*ps*	ps	as in ships
Ω	ω	omega	*ō*	o	as in obey

*At the end of words

SPECIAL RULES FOR THE TRANSLITERATION AND MODERN PRONUNCIATION OF THE GREEK LANGUAGE

COMBINATIONS OF CONSONANTS

Small Letter	Greek Names	Trans-literation	Phonetic Sound	Example
γγ	gamma + gamma	*gg*	g	as in go
γκ	gamma + kappa	*gk*	g	as in go
γχ	gamma + chi	*gch*	gh	as in ghost

DIPHTHONGS (DOUBLE VOWELS)

Small Letter	Greek Names	Trans-literation	Phonetic Sound	Example
αι	alpha + iōta	*ai*	ai	as in hair
αυ	alpha + ēpsilon	*au*	af, av	as in waft or lava
ει	epsilon + iōta	*ei*	ee	as in see
ευ	epsilon + ēpsilon	*eu*	ef, ev	as in effort or every
ηυ	ēta + ēpsilon	*ēu*	eef, eev	as in reef or sleeve
οι	omicron + iōta	*oi*	ee	as in see
ου	omicron + ēpsilon	*ou*	ou	as in group
υι	ēpsilon + iōta	*ui*	ee	as in see

BREATHINGS (Occur only with initial vowels)

(᾿) Smooth, not transliterated or pronounced.
When words begin with vowels, it may occur at the beginning of words with every vowel or double vowel (diphthong). ἔργον—*érgon*, work; εὐχή—*euchḗ*, vow.

(῾) Rough = h.
When words begin with vowels, it may occur at the beginning of words with every vowel or double vowel (diphthong). No distinction in pronunciation from the smooth breathing. To indicate the rough breathing we use "h" in the transliteration.

(ῥ) Rho = r.
(ὑ) Ēpsilon = u.
When these begin a word, they always have the rough breathing. There they are transliterated rh, hu, respectively. ῥέω—*rhéō*, flow; ὑπομονή—*hupomonḗ*, patience.

Scripture Index

John

Acts

Romans

1 Corinthians

2 Corinthians

Galatians

Ephesians

Hebrews

James

1 Peter

2 Peter

1 John

2 John

Revelation